Contents

1 Introduction: The Silent Exodus

The hushed hallways, the empty desks—these are the silent symbols of a growing crisis. Truancy. It's more than just skipping school; it's a quiet exodus, a retreat from a place that, for many, has become a source of anxiety, disconnection, or even pain. We see the numbers, the statistics that quantify the problem, but what we often miss are the stories behind those numbers. The whispered anxieties, the unspoken struggles that drive students away from the very institution designed to nurture their growth. This book isn't about judgment or blame. It's about understanding the complex tapestry of reasons that lead a student to choose absence over presence, silence over participation. It's about recognizing truancy not as a defiant act, but as a symptom of deeper, often unaddressed, needs.

Truancy isn't a singular, easily defined issue. It's a multifaceted phenomenon, influenced by a complex interplay of factors. Think of it as a ripple effect, starting from the individual student and extending outward to encompass family dynamics, peer relationships, community influences, and the overall school environment. For some, school becomes a pressure cooker of academic expectations, a place where the fear of failure overshadows the joy of learning. For others, it's a social battlefield, a landscape of isolation and bullying where the simple act of walking through the hallways feels like navigating a minefield. And for still others, the challenges extend beyond the school walls, rooted in the realities of poverty, unstable home lives, or a lack of access to essential resources. To truly address truancy, we need to peel back the layers, to understand the unique circumstances that contribute to each student's experience.

Consider the student who consistently arrives late to class, their eyes shadowed with exhaustion. Perhaps they're working a late-night job to help support their family, sacrificing sleep and study time to meet financial needs. Or imagine the student who withdraws from classroom discussions, their silence masking a deep-seated social anxiety that makes participation feel impossible. Each absence, each late arrival, each withdrawn silence tells a story. These stories, often whispered or left untold, reveal a critical truth: truancy is rarely a simple act of rebellion. It's often a cry for help, a desperate attempt to cope with overwhelming pressures and unmet needs.

This book is a journey into the heart of these silent struggles. We will explore the various factors that contribute to truancy, moving beyond simplistic explanations to examine the nuanced realities of students' lives. We'll delve into the academic pressures that can crush a student's spirit, the social dynamics that can lead to isolation and despair, and the family and community challenges that can create insurmountable barriers to education. We will hear directly from students, giving voice to their experiences and amplifying their calls for change. Their stories, shared with courage and vulnerability, offer invaluable insights into the complex emotions and challenges that underlie truancy.

This understanding is the first step towards creating meaningful solutions. We can't address a problem we don't fully comprehend. By listening to student voices, by acknowledging the systemic issues that contribute to their struggles, we can begin to build bridges of support and create pathways back to engagement. This book isn't just about identifying the problems; it's about fostering a sense of empathy and understanding. It's about shifting our perspective from seeing truancy as a disciplinary issue to recognizing it as a call for connection, a plea for support.

We will explore the impact of rigid academic structures that prioritize standardized testing over individual learning styles. We'll examine the role of zero-tolerance policies that often punish students without addressing the root causes of their behavior. And we'll delve into the critical need for trauma-informed approaches that recognize the impact of adverse childhood experiences on learning and behavior. This book challenges us to rethink our traditional approaches to school discipline and attendance, encouraging us to move towards more holistic, supportive, and student-centered models.

This book is a call to action, a plea for a more compassionate and understanding approach to truancy. It's an invitation to move beyond judgment and to engage in meaningful dialogue with students, families, and communities. It's a reminder that behind every empty desk, behind every hushed hallway, there's a story waiting to be heard. And by listening to these stories, by understanding the root causes of truancy, we can begin to create schools that are truly inclusive, supportive, and empowering for all students. This is a journey of understanding, a search for solutions, and a testament to the resilience of young people facing extraordinary challenges. It's a call to build bridges of connection and to create a future where every student feels seen, heard, and valued within the school community. This book aims to ignite a conversation, to inspire action, and to create a path forward that leaves no student behind.

1.1   Defining the Void

Truancy isn't just about skipping school. It's about the absence of something deeper, a void that goes beyond the empty desks and hushed hallways. This void can manifest in many ways: a gnawing sense of loneliness, a crushing weight of anxiety, or a simmering anger that finds no healthy outlet. It's a disconnect, a feeling of not belonging, of being unseen and unheard. For some, the void might be filled with the echoing silence of an empty home, for others, the cacophony of a chaotic one.

It's a complex, deeply personal experience, and understanding it is the first step towards bridging the gap between the student and the classroom. Imagine a puzzle with a missing piece. That piece represents the connection a student should feel to their school, their community, and even themselves. Truancy is the visible manifestation of that missing piece, the outward sign of an internal struggle.

This void is not simply a product of individual failings. It's often a reflection of larger systemic issues, the cracks in our social fabric that leave some young people feeling adrift. Think about the pressure to succeed, the fear of falling short in a world that often feels hyper-competitive. Consider the insidious nature of bullying, the isolating sting of social rejection, and the pervasive anxiety that can accompany navigating the complexities of adolescence. These pressures can be overwhelming, leaving some teens feeling like they're drowning in a sea of expectations, desperately seeking a life raft in any form. Sometimes, that life raft takes the shape of truancy, a desperate attempt to escape the overwhelming currents of their lives.

This sense of disconnection can also stem from a lack of resources and support. Imagine growing up in a community where opportunities are scarce, where poverty casts a long shadow over every aspect of life. In such environments, education can feel like a luxury, a distant dream rather than a tangible path to a better future. For some students, the immediate needs of survival - food, shelter, and safety - eclipse the long-term benefits of attending school. The void, in these cases, is filled with the harsh realities of economic hardship, making it difficult to focus on anything beyond the present moment. This isn't about a lack of ambition; it's about a fundamental lack of access and opportunity.

The void can also be a space of unmet emotional needs. Consider the impact of unstable or unhealthy family dynamics. For some, home isn't a haven, but a battleground, a place of constant stress and uncertainty. School, then, becomes not a place of learning, but an escape, a temporary respite from the turmoil. Alternatively, home might be a place of crushing responsibility, where young people are forced to take on adult roles, caring for siblings or contributing financially. In these situations, the demands of family life can eclipse the importance of education, creating a void filled with worry and obligation.

Recognizing the multifaceted nature of this void is crucial. We must move beyond simplistic explanations and address the underlying causes of truancy. This requires a shift in perspective, a move away from blaming individuals and towards understanding the complex web of factors that contribute to their disengagement. It's about recognizing the signs, listening to the whispers in the hallways, and reaching out to those students who are lost in the shadows. This book aims to illuminate these hidden corners, to give voice to the silent struggles of students, and to offer a roadmap for building bridges of connection and support. It's about filling the void with understanding, empathy, and a genuine commitment to creating a more inclusive and supportive educational landscape. It's about recognizing that behind every empty desk, there's a story waiting to be heard. And within every whispered hall, there's a cry for help, a yearning for connection, a desperate search for belonging.

1.2   Beyond the Numbers

Truancy isn't just about empty desks. It's about the silent stories hidden within those absences, the whispers echoing in the hallways long after the bell has rung. It's about the invisible struggles students face, struggles that often go unnoticed amidst the daily churn of school life. We see the numbers, the statistics on attendance rates and dropout percentages, but those numbers don't tell the whole story. They don't reveal the complex web of factors that can lead a student to disconnect from school, to choose absence over presence. To truly understand truancy, we need to look beyond the surface, beyond the simple act of not showing up. We need to delve into the lives of these students, to listen to their experiences, and to understand the world from their perspective.

Consider the student who feels like an outsider, lost in the vastness of a crowded school. They might be struggling with social anxiety, feeling invisible and unheard amidst the clamor of their peers. For them, school can feel like a constant reminder of their social isolation, a place where they don't belong. Or perhaps it's a student grappling with a learning disability that makes it difficult to keep up with the demands of the curriculum. They may feel overwhelmed and discouraged, leading them to avoid a place that reinforces their feelings of inadequacy. The pressure to succeed can be crushing, and for some, the fear of failure becomes so overwhelming that it's easier to stay away altogether.

Think about the student who carries the weight of responsibilities at home, caring for younger siblings or contributing financially to the family. For them, school might feel like a luxury they can't afford, a competing demand on their already limited time and energy. The pressures of their home life can eclipse the importance of education, leading them to prioritize immediate needs over long-term goals. These students are not simply skipping school; they are making difficult choices in challenging circumstances.

The reasons behind truancy are rarely simple. They are often deeply intertwined with a student's emotional well-being, family dynamics, and community context. A student might be experiencing bullying, struggling with mental health challenges, or grappling with difficult family situations. These challenges can make it incredibly difficult, even impossible, to focus on school. For these students, truancy is not a choice, but a consequence of circumstances beyond their control. Imagine a student living in poverty, lacking access to basic resources like stable housing, nutritious food, or reliable transportation. These challenges can create significant barriers to education, making it difficult for students to attend school regularly. They might be preoccupied with worries about where their next meal will come from or how they will get to school, making it hard to concentrate on academics. For them, truancy is a symptom of a larger systemic issue, a reflection of the inequities that exist within our communities.

Understanding the multifaceted nature of truancy is crucial to addressing it effectively. We need to move beyond simplistic explanations and punitive measures, and instead focus on creating supportive environments that address the underlying causes of student disengagement. This requires a shift in perspective, from viewing truancy as a disciplinary issue to seeing it as a cry for help. It means recognizing that behind every absence, there is a story waiting to be heard.

To truly support these students, we need to create schools that are not only places of learning, but also havens of safety and belonging. Schools where students feel seen, heard, and valued. Schools where they can access the resources and support they need to overcome challenges and thrive. This involves fostering strong relationships between students and teachers, providing access to mental health services, and creating inclusive school cultures that celebrate diversity and promote respect.

It also requires engaging with families and communities to address the broader social and economic factors that contribute to truancy. This means working with community organizations to provide resources and support to families in need, and advocating for policies that address poverty, inequality, and other systemic issues. By taking a holistic approach, we can create a network of support that empowers students to succeed, both inside and outside the classroom. Ultimately, addressing truancy is about more than just getting students back in school; it's about creating a system that truly supports their well-being and empowers them to reach their full potential. It's about recognizing that every student deserves the opportunity to learn, to grow, and to belong. It's about understanding that empty desks are not just empty spaces; they are symbols of unmet needs and unheard voices.

1.3   A Call for Understanding

Truancy isn't simply about skipping school. It's a complex issue with roots tangled deep within the lives of young people. It's a silent cry for help, a desperate attempt to escape overwhelming pressures, or a symptom of a deeper disconnect. Understanding this requires us to look beyond the empty desks and whispered hallways, to truly see the individuals behind the absences. We must shift our focus from judgment and punishment to empathy and support. This requires a fundamental shift in perspective, one that acknowledges the multifaceted nature of truancy and seeks to address the underlying causes rather than merely treating the symptoms. It's about recognizing that each absent student carries a unique story, a combination of experiences and challenges that contribute to their disengagement from school.

Imagine a student struggling with undiagnosed learning differences. They sit in class, the words blurring on the page, the teacher's voice a distant hum. Every day is a struggle, a constant reminder of their perceived inadequacy. The classroom becomes a place of anxiety and frustration, not learning and growth. For this student, truancy might be a way to avoid the daily humiliation of feeling lost and confused. It's not about defiance; it's about self-preservation. Understanding their struggle requires recognizing the invisible barriers they face and providing appropriate support. This might involve specialized tutoring, accommodations for their learning differences, or simply a compassionate teacher who understands their challenges.

Consider another scenario: a student grappling with social anxiety. The hallways feel like a minefield, every interaction a potential source of embarrassment or rejection. Lunchtime is a lonely ordeal, and the thought of participating in class discussions sends shivers down their spine. For this student, school becomes a place of fear and isolation. Truancy offers a temporary reprieve from the constant social pressure. It's a retreat, a way to protect themselves from the perceived dangers of social interaction. Addressing this requires fostering a more inclusive and supportive school environment, one where students feel safe and accepted for who they are. This could involve peer support groups, anti-bullying initiatives, or simply creating spaces where students can connect with others who share their interests.

Family dynamics also play a significant role. A teenager caring for a sick parent or younger siblings might miss school to fulfill those responsibilities. The weight of these obligations can be overwhelming, forcing them to choose between their family and their education. In these situations, truancy is not a choice but a necessity, a reflection of the difficult circumstances they face. Supporting these students requires recognizing their challenges and providing resources to alleviate their burdens. This might involve connecting families with social services, offering flexible learning options, or providing after-school care for younger siblings.

Furthermore, community factors can contribute to chronic absenteeism. Students living in poverty might lack access to basic necessities like transportation, adequate clothing, or even regular meals. These challenges can make it incredibly difficult to attend school regularly, creating a cycle of disadvantage that can be hard to break. Addressing these issues requires a community-wide effort to ensure that all students have access to the resources they need to succeed in school. This might involve providing free or subsidized transportation, school supplies, and meal programs, as well as addressing systemic issues of poverty and inequality.

The reasons behind truancy are as diverse as the students themselves. There is no one-size-fits-all explanation, and there is no simple solution. Understanding this requires us to listen to the voices of these young people, to hear their stories, and to acknowledge their struggles. It means recognizing that behind every absence is a complex individual deserving of our empathy and support. It means creating schools that are not just places of learning, but also havens of belonging, where every student feels seen, heard, and valued. It means fostering a culture of understanding, where we move beyond judgment and punishment and embrace the opportunity to help these young people find their way back to connection, engagement, and a sense of purpose. It means recognizing that addressing truancy is not just about getting students back in school; it's about addressing the underlying issues that led them to leave in the first place. It's about creating a system that supports the whole child, not just their academic performance. It's about building a future where every student has the opportunity to thrive.

2 The Pressure Cooker: Academic Stress

The relentless pursuit of good grades, the pressure to outperform peers, the looming shadow of standardized tests – these are just a few of the stressors that contribute to the immense academic pressure faced by today's students. This pressure, often originating from a combination of external sources and internal anxieties, can manifest in a variety of ways. Think about the weight of parental expectations. For some, it's the subtle but constant push for higher achievement, the unspoken disappointment in anything less than perfect. For others, it's the overt pressure to follow a specific career path, regardless of personal interests or aptitudes. This external pressure can quickly internalize, transforming into a crippling fear of failure.

Imagine waking up each morning with a knot in your stomach, dreading the day ahead. The upcoming test, the daunting pile of homework, the fear of not measuring up – these anxieties can become all-consuming. School, once a place of learning and growth, can transform into a source of constant stress and anxiety. This chronic stress can lead to physical symptoms like headaches, stomachaches, and sleep disturbances. Mentally, it can manifest as difficulty concentrating, increased irritability, and a pervasive sense of overwhelm. For some students, this pressure cooker environment becomes so unbearable that they begin to withdraw, seeking escape through truancy.

The fear of failure is a powerful motivator, but not always in a positive way. It can paralyze students, preventing them from taking risks or even trying. The thought of a bad grade, a failed test, or disappointing a parent can be so overwhelming that it becomes easier to avoid the situation altogether. This avoidance can take many forms, from feigning illness to simply skipping class. The irony is that while avoiding school might provide temporary relief from the pressure, it ultimately exacerbates the problem. Falling behind in coursework only increases the anxiety and makes it even harder to return. This creates a vicious cycle of avoidance and increasing pressure, further isolating the student from the very support systems they need.

Consider the impact of a competitive academic environment. In some schools, the pressure to excel is palpable, creating a culture of comparison and competition. Students are constantly measured against their peers, creating a sense of inadequacy and fear of falling behind. This hyper-competitive atmosphere can be particularly damaging for students who struggle academically or who learn at a different pace. They may feel like they are constantly playing catch-up, further fueling their anxiety and sense of failure. This pressure to perform can also lead to unhealthy coping mechanisms, such as cheating or substance abuse, as students desperately seek ways to alleviate the stress.

The constant pressure to achieve academically can also stifle a student's natural curiosity and love of learning. When the focus is solely on grades and test scores, the joy of discovery and the intrinsic motivation to learn can be lost. Students may become disengaged from their studies, viewing school as a chore rather than an opportunity for growth. This can lead to a sense of apathy and resentment, further contributing to truancy. It is crucial to remember that education is not solely about academic achievement. It is about developing well-rounded individuals who are equipped with the skills and knowledge to navigate the complexities of life.

The emphasis on standardized tests further adds to the pressure cooker environment. These high-stakes exams, often seen as the sole measure of a student's worth, can create immense anxiety and pressure to perform. The pressure to achieve a certain score can be overwhelming, leading to sleepless nights, intense studying, and a constant fear of not measuring up. This pressure is particularly acute for students from disadvantaged backgrounds who may lack access to the resources and support needed to succeed on these tests. The fear of not performing well on these tests can be a major factor in student truancy.

The pressure to get into a "good" college further intensifies the academic pressure cooker. From a young age, students are told that their future depends on getting into a prestigious university. This pressure can lead to an unhealthy obsession with grades, test scores, and extracurricular activities, often at the expense of their well-being and mental health. The college application process itself can be incredibly stressful, with students facing intense competition and uncertainty about their future. This pressure can be particularly challenging for students who are the first in their families to apply to college or who come from under-resourced communities.

Beyond the external pressures, internal factors also contribute to academic stress. Perfectionism, a common trait among high-achieving students, can be a double-edged sword. While striving for excellence is admirable, the relentless pursuit of perfection can be debilitating. Perfectionists often set unrealistic standards for themselves and experience intense self-criticism when they fall short. This constant self-doubt and fear of making mistakes can lead to anxiety, procrastination, and a reluctance to take risks. It's essential for students to learn to embrace imperfection and to recognize that mistakes are a natural part of the learning process.

It's important to remember that seeking help is not a sign of weakness but a sign of strength. Talking to a trusted adult - a parent, teacher, counselor, or mentor - can provide invaluable support and guidance. These individuals can offer a listening ear, practical advice, and resources to help manage academic stress. They can also help students develop healthy coping mechanisms, such as time management skills, stress reduction techniques, and strategies for overcoming procrastination. By addressing the root causes of academic stress and providing students with the support they need, we can create a more positive and nurturing learning environment that fosters growth, resilience, and a genuine love of learning.

2.1 The Weight of Expectations

The weight of expectations can feel like an invisible backpack, constantly adding books, assignments, and pressures until it's almost too heavy to bear. It's not just about grades. For some, it's the pressure to live up to parental dreams, the unspoken competition with siblings, or the constant comparisons to classmates. The desire to succeed can morph into a fear of failure so intense that it paralyzes you. School, a place meant for learning and growth, becomes a source of anxiety and dread. This constant pressure can manifest in different ways. Some students become withdrawn and quiet, losing interest in activities they once enjoyed. Others might act out, becoming disruptive or even defiant. Sleepless nights spent worrying about upcoming tests or presentations become the norm. Stomach aches and headaches become frequent companions. This isn't just typical teenage angst; this is the tangible weight of expectations impacting physical and mental well-being.

Imagine carrying a stack of heavy textbooks, one for every class, every expectation, every whispered comparison. Each book represents a different pressure – the perfect GPA, the athletic scholarship, the lead in the school play, the acceptance into a prestigious college. Now imagine trying to run a race carrying that weight. That's what it feels like to navigate adolescence under the crushing weight of expectations. You're constantly trying to move forward, to achieve and succeed, but the burden slows you down, making each step a struggle. The pressure can be internal, stemming from a personal drive for perfection. It can be external, fueled by parental ambitions or societal standards. Often, it's a combination of both, creating a relentless cycle of pressure that can feel inescapable.

This pressure cooker environment often leads to unhealthy coping mechanisms. Some students might seek solace in unhealthy habits, like excessive screen time, overeating, or substance use, as a way to escape the constant pressure. Others might develop unhealthy perfectionist tendencies, pushing themselves to the brink of exhaustion in pursuit of unattainable standards. This relentless pursuit of achievement can also lead to a fear of taking risks. Students might avoid challenging themselves academically or socially, fearing that any misstep will shatter the carefully constructed image of success they've built for themselves and others.

It's important to recognize that these expectations, while sometimes well-intentioned, can have a detrimental effect. The constant pressure to achieve can stifle creativity, curiosity, and the natural joy of learning. School becomes a chore, a source of stress, rather than a place of discovery and growth. The focus shifts from learning and personal development to simply meeting external expectations, no matter the personal cost. This shift can have long-term consequences, impacting a student's self-esteem, mental health, and overall well-being.

One of the most insidious consequences of the weight of expectations is the feeling of isolation. Students might feel they can't talk about their struggles, fearing judgment or disappointment from those who have placed these expectations upon them. They might believe they are the only ones experiencing these pressures, further deepening their sense of loneliness. This isolation can be particularly damaging for teenagers, who are already navigating the complex social and emotional landscape of adolescence. The feeling of being alone in their struggles can exacerbate anxiety and depression, making it even harder to cope with the weight of expectations.

Breaking free from this cycle requires a multifaceted approach. It starts with open communication. Talk to your parents, teachers, counselors, or trusted friends about how you're feeling. Share the weight you're carrying. Often, simply voicing your struggles can be a powerful first step towards finding relief. Remember, seeking help is a sign of strength, not weakness. It takes courage to admit you're struggling and to reach out for support. It's essential to cultivate self-compassion. Recognize that you are human, and it's okay to make mistakes. Learning from setbacks is part of the growth process. Focus on your efforts and progress rather than solely on the end result. Celebrate your achievements, no matter how small, and acknowledge the hard work you've put in along the way.

Reframing your perspective on success is crucial. Success isn't just about grades or external validation. It's about personal growth, resilience, and the pursuit of your passions. Define success on your own terms, based on your values and goals, not on the expectations of others. This shift in perspective can significantly reduce the pressure you feel and allow you to focus on what truly matters to you. Remember, your worth is not defined by your academic achievements or external accomplishments. You are valuable simply for being you.

Learning to manage stress effectively is another vital component of navigating the weight of expectations. Explore healthy coping mechanisms, such as exercise, mindfulness, spending time in nature, or pursuing creative outlets. These activities can help you manage stress, improve your mood, and foster a sense of well-being. Find what works best for you and incorporate these practices into your daily routine. Prioritize your mental and physical health. Get enough sleep, eat nutritious foods, and engage in activities that bring you joy. Taking care of your well-being is not selfish; it's essential for navigating the challenges of adolescence and building resilience.

The weight of expectations can be heavy, but it doesn't have to be a defining factor in your life. By communicating openly, cultivating self-compassion, reframing your perspective on success, and prioritizing your well-being, you can navigate these pressures and find your own path, one that is defined by your unique strengths, passions, and aspirations. Remember, you are not alone in this journey, and there is support available.

2.2 Fear of Failure

The weight of a bad grade can feel crushing. It can feel like a defining moment, a label that sticks. One failing test, one missed assignment, and suddenly you're convinced you're not smart enough. This fear of failure, this deep-seated anxiety about not measuring up, can be paralyzing. It can make you want to avoid school altogether, to escape the potential for disappointment, the scrutiny of teachers, the whispers of classmates. But avoiding school, avoiding the challenge, only reinforces the fear. It creates a vicious cycle where the fear becomes the reality. Think about a time you were really afraid of something, like speaking in public or trying out for a team. The anticipation, the knot in your stomach, the racing heart—those feelings are intense. But what happens after you've faced that fear? Even if it didn't go perfectly, you likely felt a sense of relief, a sense of accomplishment. You proved to yourself that you could handle it. Facing your academic fears is no different. It's about taking small steps, tackling one challenge at a time. Maybe it's asking a teacher for help, studying with a friend, or breaking down a big project into smaller, more manageable pieces. Each small victory builds confidence, chipping away at the fear.

This fear often isn't about the grade itself. It's about what that grade represents. It's about feeling like you're letting yourself down, letting your parents down, not living up to expectations, real or perceived. It's about the stories we tell ourselves: "I'm not good enough," "I'm not as smart as everyone else," "I'll never succeed." These negative thoughts can become self-fulfilling prophecies. They can sap our motivation and make us give up before we've even started. Challenge those negative thoughts. Ask yourself: Is this thought really true? What evidence do I have to support it? What would I tell a friend who was having this same thought? Often, when we examine these negative thoughts more closely, we realize they're based on fear, not facts.

Remember, everyone makes mistakes. Everyone experiences setbacks. It's part of being human. It's these very setbacks that allow us to learn and grow. Think of successful people you admire. They didn't get where they are without facing challenges, without stumbling along the way. They learned from their mistakes, they picked themselves up, and they kept going. Resilience, the ability to bounce back from adversity, is a skill you can develop. It starts with recognizing that failure isn't the opposite of success; it's a stepping stone.

Sometimes, the fear of failure masks a deeper fear: the fear of vulnerability. Putting yourself out there, trying your best, and potentially not succeeding can feel incredibly exposing. It's like opening yourself up to judgment. But think about it: Vulnerability is also the birthplace of courage. It takes courage to raise your hand in class even when you're not sure you have the right answer. It takes courage to ask for help when you're struggling. It takes courage to try something new, knowing you might not be good at it right away. Embrace the vulnerability. It's a sign that you're pushing yourself, that you're growing.

Consider the alternative: living in fear, holding yourself back, never taking risks. That's not a fulfilling life. Growth happens outside your comfort zone. It happens when you're willing to embrace the possibility of failure, knowing that even if you don't succeed, you'll learn something valuable in the process. And who knows? You might surprise yourself. You might discover hidden talents and strengths you never knew you had. Don't let fear hold you back from exploring your potential.

So, how do you break free from this cycle of fear? Start by acknowledging it. Don't try to suppress or ignore the feeling. Name it. Say to yourself, "I'm feeling afraid of failing this test." Just acknowledging the fear can take away some of its power. Then, ask yourself: What's the worst that could happen? Realistically, what are the consequences of not doing well on this test, this assignment, this project? Often, the worst-case scenario isn't nearly as bad as we imagine.

Next, focus on what you can control. You can't control the outcome, but you can control your preparation. You can control how much effort you put in, how much time you dedicate to studying, how you approach the challenge. Focus on the process, not the result. Focus on learning and growing, not just on getting a good grade. The more you focus on what you can control, the less power the fear will have over you. Remember, you are not defined by your grades. You are defined by your character, your resilience, your willingness to learn and grow. Embrace the challenge. Embrace the learning process. And don't be afraid to ask for help. There are people who care about you and want to see you succeed. Reach out to them. Let them support you. You don't have to face this alone.

3 Lost in the Crowd: Social Isolation

The hallways buzz with activity, lockers slam, and laughter echoes. Yet, amid this vibrant scene, some students remain invisible, lost in the crowd. They navigate the school day like ghosts, unnoticed and unheard. This experience of social isolation, of feeling disconnected and unseen, is a powerful undercurrent in the lives of many truant teens. It's a chilling paradox: surrounded by people yet utterly alone. This sense of isolation isn't simply about being alone; it's about feeling emotionally detached, like an outsider looking in. It's a pervasive feeling of not belonging, of not having a place within the social fabric of the school. This feeling can be incredibly debilitating, draining motivation and fostering a sense of despair. For some, the school environment, rather than being a place of connection, becomes a constant reminder of their social disconnection.

The desire for connection is a fundamental human need. We crave acceptance, understanding, and a sense of belonging. When these needs aren't met, it can create a deep sense of unease and insecurity. For teenagers, navigating the already complex social landscape of adolescence, this unmet need can be particularly challenging. School, ideally a space for social development and connection, can become a source of anxiety and avoidance for those struggling to find their place. This struggle is often internalized, making it difficult for others to recognize the pain beneath the surface. Students experiencing social isolation may appear withdrawn, quiet, or even disinterested, but beneath this exterior lies a yearning for connection and acceptance.

Bullying, in all its forms, exacerbates this feeling of isolation. Whether it's physical intimidation, verbal abuse, or the insidious whispers of social exclusion, bullying creates a hostile environment that further isolates its victims. It chips away at their self-worth, making them feel unworthy of connection and belonging. The constant fear and anxiety associated with bullying can make school a place of dread, a place to be avoided at all costs. This avoidance, while a coping mechanism, further reinforces the cycle of isolation, making it even harder to break free. The scars of bullying run deep, impacting not just the present but also the student's ability to form healthy relationships in the future.

The search for a "tribe," a group of peers who share similar interests and values, is a crucial part of adolescence. This search for belonging is a natural and healthy process, but for some, it can be a frustrating and isolating experience. The pressure to conform, to fit into a particular social group, can be immense. When students feel like they don't fit in anywhere, it can intensify their sense of isolation. This feeling of not belonging can lead to a loss of self-esteem and a sense of hopelessness. It's essential for teenagers to understand that finding their tribe takes time and that it's okay to be different. Authenticity, embracing their unique qualities, is key to attracting genuine connections.

The online world can offer a seemingly safe haven for socially isolated teens. It provides a space to connect with others who share similar interests, regardless of geographical location. Online communities can offer a sense of belonging and validation that may be lacking in the offline world. However, this online oasis can also be a double-edged sword. While it can provide a sense of connection, it can also become a source of further isolation. Excessive online engagement can lead to a detachment from the real world, replacing face-to-face interactions with virtual ones. The curated nature of online profiles can also create unrealistic expectations and intensify feelings of inadequacy. Finding a healthy balance between online and offline connections is crucial for well-being.

The experience of socially isolated students often goes unnoticed. They become the "invisible students," the ones who blend into the background, their struggles hidden beneath a veneer of normalcy. Their silence often masks a deep sense of loneliness and despair. It's crucial for educators, parents, and peers to be attuned to the subtle signs of social isolation. A quiet student, a withdrawn demeanor, or a sudden change in behavior can all be indicators of a deeper struggle. Creating a school environment where every student feels seen, heard, and valued is paramount. Fostering a culture of empathy, kindness, and inclusion can make a profound difference in the lives of those struggling with social isolation. Reaching out, offering a listening ear, and extending a hand of friendship can be the first steps towards breaking down the walls of loneliness and helping these students find their place.

3.1   The Struggle for Connection

The hallways can feel like a vast, echoing wilderness when you're navigating them alone. Lunchtime can morph into an agonizing exercise in invisibility, spent shuffling trays and avoiding eye contact. Classes can become a blur of faces, none of which seem to register you. This is the reality for many teens struggling with social disconnection at school, a silent battle fought within the crowded halls. It's a struggle that can be just as debilitating as any academic challenge, and it can be a powerful driver of truancy.

For some, the disconnect stems from a lack of established friendships. Starting at a new school, moving to a different town, or simply drifting apart from old friends can leave a gaping hole in a teen's social fabric. This absence of a familiar support system can make school feel overwhelmingly alienating. The fear of approaching new people, the insecurity of not knowing where to fit in, can be paralyzing. These feelings can escalate, making even the thought of walking through the school doors a source of immense anxiety.

The experience of bullying further complicates the struggle for connection. While not all students who experience social isolation are bullied, the two often go hand in hand. Being targeted by bullies can shatter a teenager's sense of self-worth and safety, making school feel like a hostile environment. The constant threat of verbal or physical abuse creates a hyper-vigilance that drains energy and makes it difficult to focus on learning or social interaction. This constant stress can lead to avoidance behaviors, including truancy, as a means of self-preservation.

Even in the absence of overt bullying, the subtle pressures of social hierarchies and the pervasive fear of not fitting in can be intensely isolating. Teenagers are acutely aware of social dynamics, constantly evaluating their own position within the complex web of peer relationships. The desire to belong, to be accepted by a group, is a fundamental human need, and its absence can be profoundly painful. This yearning for connection can sometimes lead teens down unhealthy paths, chasing acceptance from groups that might not have their best interests at heart.

The rise of social media adds another layer of complexity to the struggle for connection. While online platforms can offer opportunities for connection and community, they can also exacerbate feelings of isolation and inadequacy. The curated perfection of online profiles can create unrealistic expectations and fuel social comparisons, leaving teens feeling like they don't measure up. The constant barrage of images and updates can also amplify feelings of FOMO (fear of missing out), further isolating those who are already struggling to connect offline.

This sense of disconnection can manifest in various ways. Some students become withdrawn and quiet, fading into the background of classroom life. Others might act out, seeking attention through disruptive behavior. Still others might try to disappear altogether, resorting to truancy as a way to escape the social pressures and anxieties of school. They may find temporary solace in solitude, but this avoidance ultimately reinforces their isolation and further disconnects them from the support systems that school can provide.

It's crucial to remember that behind every act of truancy, there's a story. There's a student struggling with something, whether it's academic pressure, social isolation, family issues, or a combination of factors. Understanding these underlying struggles is the first step towards offering effective support. Creating a school environment where every student feels seen, heard, and valued is essential to fostering genuine connection. This involves cultivating a culture of kindness and empathy, where students feel safe to express themselves and reach out for help. It requires proactive efforts to identify and support students who are struggling with social isolation, providing them with opportunities to build meaningful relationships and develop a sense of belonging. This might involve peer mentoring programs, social skills groups, or simply creating more inclusive social spaces within the school.

Remember, the struggle for connection is real, and it's impacting countless teens. By acknowledging this struggle and working together to create more supportive and inclusive school communities, we can help students find their place, build resilience, and thrive. This isn't just about improving attendance; it's about fostering well-being and empowering students to reach their full potential. Recognizing the silent struggles happening within our schools is the first step towards building a more connected and compassionate future for all.

3.2 Bullying's Shadow

The sting of exclusion, the fear that clenches your stomach before walking into the cafeteria, the constant looking-over-your-shoulder – these are the shadows cast by bullying. It's a chilling reality for many students, a constant undercurrent of anxiety that can make school feel less like a place of learning and more like a battleground. This isn't about the occasional teasing or playground spat. We're talking about sustained, targeted harassment – physical, verbal, or emotional – that chips away at a person's self-worth and sense of safety. It's the insidious whisper campaign, the online ridicule, the deliberate social isolation that can leave a young person feeling utterly alone and vulnerable.

Bullying weaves itself into the fabric of a student's life, impacting every aspect of their school experience. Academically, the stress and anxiety can make it difficult to concentrate, leading to declining grades and a growing sense of disengagement. Socially, the fear of further harassment can lead to withdrawal, making it harder to form friendships and find a sense of belonging. The school environment, once a place of potential and growth, becomes a source of dread. This fear, this constant state of alert, can manifest physically too - stomachaches, headaches, sleep disturbances - further compounding the problem and reinforcing the desire to stay away.

It's crucial to understand that bullying thrives on silence. The bully's power is amplified when their actions go unchecked, when the target feels they have nowhere to turn. This silence can be born out of fear - fear of retaliation, fear of not being believed, or even fear of making the situation worse. Sometimes, it's a sense of shame that keeps students from speaking up. They may internalize the bullying, believing that they somehow deserve the treatment they are receiving. This self-blame can be incredibly damaging, eroding their self-esteem and further isolating them.

Breaking this silence is the first step towards reclaiming power. Talking to a trusted adult - a parent, teacher, counselor, or other mentor - is essential. These individuals can provide support, guidance, and practical strategies for navigating the situation. They can also help to advocate for the student within the school system, ensuring that the bullying is addressed and that appropriate measures are taken. Remember, you don't have to face this alone. There are people who care and who want to help.

Beyond seeking help from adults, finding supportive peers can make a profound difference. Connecting with others who understand what you're going through can provide a sense of validation and belonging. Support groups, clubs, or even just a few close friends can offer a safe space to share experiences, build resilience, and regain a sense of community. Knowing that you're not alone in this struggle can be incredibly empowering.

Addressing bullying requires a multi-faceted approach. Schools need to foster a culture of respect and inclusivity, where bullying is not tolerated and where students feel safe reporting incidents without fear of reprisal. This involves implementing clear anti-bullying policies, providing training for staff and students, and creating opportunities for open dialogue about the issue. It's not enough to simply react to incidents of bullying; schools need to proactively create an environment where bullying is less likely to occur in the first place.

For students experiencing bullying, remember that your feelings are valid. The pain, the fear, the anger - these are all natural responses to a deeply hurtful experience. Allow yourself to feel these emotions, but don't let them define you. Focus on building your resilience, on finding healthy coping mechanisms, and on surrounding yourself with supportive people. Whether it's through journaling, creative expression, spending time in nature, or engaging in activities you enjoy, find what helps you to process your emotions and regain a sense of control. Your well-being is paramount, and taking care of yourself is a crucial part of navigating this challenging time.

Finally, it's important to remember that healing takes time. There's no quick fix, no magic wand that will erase the impact of bullying overnight. Be patient with yourself, celebrate small victories, and never give up on finding your place, your voice, and your sense of belonging. The shadows of bullying can be long, but they don't have to define you. With support, resilience, and a belief in your own worth, you can emerge from the darkness and step into the light. You are stronger than you think, and you deserve to feel safe, respected, and valued.

3.3 Finding Your Tribe

School can feel like a vast, echoing space when you're lost in the crowd. You see the clusters of friends, the inside jokes, the shared laughter, and you're on the outside looking in. This feeling of isolation can be one of the most powerful drivers of truancy. It's not about skipping school; it's about escaping a place where you feel invisible, unheard, and disconnected. The good news is that finding your tribe, your group, your people, is possible, even if it doesn't feel that way right now. It takes time, effort, and a willingness to step outside your comfort zone, but the reward of belonging is worth it.

Start by identifying your interests. What are you passionate about? What activities make you lose track of time? Whether it's art, music, sports, gaming, coding, or anything else, focusing on your interests is a powerful way to connect with like-minded individuals. Look for clubs, organizations, or groups related to these interests, both inside and outside of school. Community centers, libraries, and local organizations often offer a wide range of activities. This provides a natural starting point for conversations and connections, built around a shared passion. Don't limit yourself to just one area. Explore different avenues, try new things. You might be surprised at where you find your niche. Maybe you've always loved animals - volunteering at a local animal shelter could introduce you to a whole community of compassionate animal lovers. Perhaps you're fascinated by history - joining a historical society or visiting a local museum can connect you with others who share your curiosity. The point is to actively seek out opportunities that resonate with you.

Approach social interactions with a genuine curiosity about others. Ask questions, listen actively, and show a genuine interest in getting to know people. Instead of focusing on what you can get from the interaction, focus on what you can contribute. Offer a helping hand, share a kind word, or simply be present and listen. Building genuine connections takes time and effort, but it starts with showing genuine interest in others.

Don't be afraid to step outside your usual social circles. Sometimes, the people we connect with most deeply are those we least expect. Talk to the quiet kid in class, strike up a conversation with someone new at a club meeting, or even just smile at someone you pass in the hall. Small interactions can lead to bigger connections. You never know where you'll find your people, so be open to possibilities.

Remember that building meaningful connections takes time. It's not about instantly clicking with everyone you meet. It's about nurturing relationships, being patient, and allowing friendships to develop organically. Don't get discouraged if it doesn't happen overnight. Keep putting yourself out there, keep exploring, and keep believing that you will find your place.

Navigating social situations can be awkward, especially if you're feeling shy or unsure of yourself. One helpful strategy is to observe social dynamics before jumping in. Pay attention to how others interact, the flow of conversations, and the overall atmosphere of the group. This can give you a better sense of how to navigate the situation and feel more comfortable participating.

Sometimes, connecting with others starts with connecting with yourself. Understanding your own values, interests, and strengths can give you a stronger sense of self and make it easier to connect with others who share similar qualities. Reflect on what's important to you, what makes you unique, and what you bring to the table. This self-awareness can be a powerful tool in building authentic connections.

Don't underestimate the power of shared experiences. Participating in group activities, whether it's a school project, a community event, or even just playing a game together, can create a sense of camaraderie and connection. Working towards a common goal, sharing a challenge, or simply enjoying a shared experience can forge bonds and create lasting memories.

Remember that finding your tribe is not about conforming to be like everyone else. It's about finding people who appreciate you for who you are, quirks and all. Embrace your individuality, be authentic, and don't be afraid to let your true self shine. The right people will connect with the real you, not a version of yourself you think they want to see. It's important to recognize that not every group will be the right fit. Sometimes, you might find yourself in a situation where you don't feel comfortable or accepted. It's okay to move on and continue your search. Finding your tribe is about finding a place where you feel valued, respected, and supported. Don't settle for anything less.

Finally, remember that you're not alone in this journey. Many students feel lost and disconnected at some point in their school experience. Reach out to a trusted adult, a counselor, or a teacher if you're struggling. They can offer support, guidance, and resources to help you find your place and connect with others.

3.4   The Online Oasis

For some, the hushed hallways and empty desks represent a terrifying isolation. But for others, the quiet solitude of truancy is a welcome escape, traded for the vibrant, albeit sometimes chaotic, buzz of online communities. These digital spaces, offering connection and a sense of belonging, can become an oasis for teens navigating the turbulent waters of adolescence. They find solace in shared interests, forging friendships with individuals across geographical boundaries who understand their passions and struggles in ways their real-world peers might not. This chapter explores the complex relationship between online communities and truancy, acknowledging the potential benefits while cautioning against the pitfalls of substituting virtual connection for real-world engagement.

Online spaces offer a unique form of validation often absent in traditional school settings. Teenagers who feel marginalized or unseen in their classrooms can find platforms where their voices are heard and valued. Whether it's through fan fiction, online gaming, or creative forums, these spaces provide opportunities for self-expression and the development of unique identities. The anonymity afforded by the internet can be empowering, allowing shy or insecure teens to explore different facets of themselves without the fear of judgment or social repercussions they might experience at school. This freedom to experiment and connect with like-minded individuals can be incredibly valuable, fostering a sense of belonging that might be lacking elsewhere. However, this sense of belonging can be a double-edged sword. While online communities can provide support and friendship, they can also become a form of escapism. The curated nature of online profiles and interactions can create an idealized version of reality, one that contrasts sharply with the complexities and challenges of face-to-face relationships. The constant availability of online connection can also lead to dependence, making it difficult for teens to prioritize real-world interactions and navigate the nuances of in-person communication. The allure of these digital sanctuaries can be particularly strong for students struggling with social anxiety or bullying, leading them to retreat further into the online world and avoid the challenges of school altogether. It's crucial to recognize the distinction between healthy online engagement and unhealthy dependence. Participating in online communities that foster creativity, shared learning, and positive social interaction can be incredibly enriching. However, when these online spaces become a substitute for real-world experiences and relationships, it can hinder a teenager's social and emotional development. Excessive time spent online can lead to social isolation, difficulty forming meaningful relationships offline, and a distorted perception of social norms. It can also contribute to sleep deprivation, impacting academic performance and overall well-being.

The potential for cyberbullying adds another layer of complexity to the online landscape. While many online communities offer supportive environments, others can be breeding grounds for negativity and harassment. The anonymity that empowers some can also embolden others to engage in hurtful behavior without fear of accountability. For teens already struggling with self-esteem or social anxieties, cyberbullying can be particularly devastating, exacerbating feelings of isolation and contributing to truancy as they seek to avoid the online spaces that have become sources of pain.

Parents and educators play a vital role in helping teenagers navigate the online world safely and responsibly. Open communication and a genuine interest in a teenager's online activities can create a space for dialogue about online safety, healthy boundaries, and the importance of balancing virtual and real-world connections. Encouraging teens to pursue their interests online while also fostering offline social connections can help them reap the benefits of digital communities without sacrificing the crucial developmental experiences of face-to-face interaction. It's about fostering a healthy relationship with technology, one that enhances rather than hinders their overall well-being.

Furthermore, recognizing the underlying reasons why a teen might be seeking solace online is crucial. If a student is experiencing bullying, social isolation, or academic pressure at school, addressing these root causes is essential. Simply restricting online access without providing alternative avenues for connection and support can be counterproductive, pushing the teen further into isolation. Creating supportive and inclusive school environments where students feel valued and accepted can lessen the allure of online escapism and encourage greater engagement with the school community.

Ultimately, understanding the role of online communities in the lives of truant teens requires a nuanced approach. It's not about demonizing technology, but about recognizing its potential for both harm and healing. By fostering open communication, promoting healthy online habits, and addressing the underlying issues that may be driving teens to seek refuge online, we can help them navigate the digital landscape safely and effectively, ensuring that the online oasis doesn't become an island of isolation.

3.5   Invisible Students

There's a particular kind of invisibility that goes beyond simply being quiet or unnoticed. It's a fading away, a slow erosion of presence within the very walls meant to nurture you. You're physically present, sitting in class, yet somehow absent. Your voice is lost in the classroom hum, your thoughts adrift, your connection to the learning process severed. You become a ghost in your own life, a student in name only. This invisibility isn't about a desire to disappear entirely, but rather a desperate coping mechanism. It's a shield erected against the anxieties and pressures of the school environment, a way to navigate a world that feels overwhelming and unwelcoming.

This sense of detachment can manifest in various ways. It might be the student who consistently sits in the back row, avoiding eye contact and participation. Perhaps they're the one who's always doodling in their notebook, their mind miles away from the lesson. Or maybe they're the student who perpetually arrives late, slips out early, or disappears for entire periods, their absences barely registering on the radar of overworked teachers. They exist in the periphery, blending into the background noise of the school day. They become adept at the art of camouflage, mastering the subtle cues that allow them to remain unseen, unheard, and ultimately, unhelped. Their invisibility becomes a self-fulfilling prophecy, further isolating them from the very connections they crave.

This invisibility is often a byproduct of deeper struggles. Perhaps it's rooted in social anxiety, a crippling fear of judgment that makes even the simplest interactions feel like a high-stakes performance. Maybe it stems from academic pressure, the relentless pursuit of achievement that leaves students feeling inadequate and overwhelmed. Or perhaps it's a consequence of bullying, the relentless taunts and harassment that erode self-worth and create an environment of fear and isolation. Whatever the underlying cause, the result is the same: a gradual disengagement from the school community, a retreat into the shadows of invisibility.

The classroom becomes a stage for their silent performance of detachment. Every question unanswered, every hand unraised, every averted gaze is a small act of self-preservation, a way to protect themselves from the perceived dangers of engagement. The school hallways become a labyrinth of anonymity, where they can navigate the crowds unnoticed, blending into the sea of faces. They exist in the liminal spaces between connection and isolation, longing for belonging but fearing the vulnerability that comes with it. Their invisibility becomes a paradox: a desperate attempt to avoid being seen, while simultaneously yearning to be recognized and understood.

Breaking free from this cycle of invisibility requires a multi-pronged approach. It demands a shift in perspective, both from the student struggling with these feelings and the adults in their lives. For the student, it often begins with acknowledging the underlying issues that contribute to their withdrawal. Recognizing the root of their invisibility, whether it's social anxiety, academic pressure, or past trauma, is the first step towards reclaiming their voice and their presence. It may involve seeking support from a counselor, therapist, or trusted adult who can provide guidance and encouragement. It requires courage to step out of the shadows and begin the process of reconnecting with themselves and the world around them.

For teachers, administrators, and parents, it's crucial to cultivate an environment of attentiveness and empathy. This means looking beyond the surface level of behavior and recognizing the subtle signs of disengagement. It means creating a classroom culture where students feel safe to take risks, ask questions, and express themselves without fear of judgment. It means fostering a sense of belonging, where every student feels valued and respected, regardless of their academic performance or social status. It requires a commitment to seeing the unseen, hearing the unheard, and reaching out to those who are silently struggling.

Ultimately, breaking the cycle of invisibility is about fostering connection. It's about creating spaces where students feel seen, heard, and understood. It's about empowering them to reclaim their voices and their place within the school community. It's about reminding them that they are not alone, that their struggles are valid, and that there is hope for a brighter future, a future where they can step out of the shadows and embrace their full potential. It's about recognizing that every student deserves to feel a sense of belonging, a sense of purpose, and a sense of hope within the walls of their school. It's about transforming the whispered halls into spaces of vibrant connection and the empty desks into seats of active engagement.

4 Home Truths: Family Dynamics

Family isn't always a Norman Rockwell painting. It's rarely perfect, often messy, and sometimes a source of immense pain. For some teens, home is anything but a safe haven. It's a battleground of constant conflict, a place of neglect, or a source of overwhelming pressure. This reality can make school, with its structure and expectations, feel unbearable, leading to truancy as a desperate attempt to escape. School might represent a predictable routine, but when home life is chaotic, even that predictability can feel suffocating.

Consider the weight a teen might carry when dealing with parents struggling with addiction or mental health issues. They may become young caregivers, shouldering responsibilities far beyond their years. Cooking meals, looking after younger siblings, managing household finances - these tasks steal time and energy, leaving little room for schoolwork, let alone social interaction. The emotional toll is even heavier. Shame, fear, and resentment can fester, creating a constant state of anxiety that makes focusing on academics nearly impossible. School becomes another burden, another source of stress in an already overflowing cup. The quiet of an empty classroom might offer temporary respite from the chaos at home, but it's a band-aid solution to a deep wound.

Sometimes, the pressure comes from a different source - unrealistic expectations. Parents, driven by their own ambitions, may push their children relentlessly towards academic achievement. Straight A's, prestigious extracurriculars, and a perfect college application become the sole focus. In these homes, anything less than perfection is seen as failure. This pressure can be crushing, leading to crippling anxiety and a fear of disappointing parents. For some teens, skipping school becomes a way to reclaim a sense of control, a silent rebellion against the suffocating pressure to achieve. It's a desperate attempt to escape the constant scrutiny and the fear of not measuring up. The school building itself can become a symbol of that pressure, a reminder of the impossible standards they feel they can never reach.

Family dynamics also play a significant role in shaping a teen's self-esteem and sense of belonging. In homes marked by constant conflict, children may internalize negative messages, believing they are somehow responsible for the dysfunction. This can erode their self-worth, making them feel unworthy of connection and belonging. School, instead of being a place of social interaction and growth, can become a painful reminder of their perceived inadequacy. They might withdraw, avoiding social situations and eventually school altogether. Truancy, in this case, is not an act of defiance but a retreat into isolation. It's a desperate attempt to protect themselves from further emotional pain.

Even in seemingly stable families, subtle dynamics can contribute to a teen's disengagement from school. A lack of emotional support, a feeling of being unseen or unheard, can leave a teenager feeling adrift. They might yearn for connection and validation, but if those needs aren't met at home, they might seek them elsewhere, perhaps in unhealthy peer groups or online communities. School, in its perceived indifference, becomes irrelevant. It fails to offer the emotional sustenance they crave, pushing them further towards the margins. The desks and hallways, once symbols of learning and opportunity, become emblems of their emotional disconnect.

Consider the impact of significant life events: divorce, the death of a loved one, or a serious illness within the family. These events can disrupt family routines and create emotional upheaval. Teenagers, already navigating the complexities of adolescence, might struggle to cope with these added stressors. School can feel overwhelming, a stark contrast to the emotional turmoil they're experiencing at home. Skipping school might offer a temporary escape, a way to avoid the demands of academic life while they grapple with personal loss or change. The school environment, with its focus on routine and achievement, can feel jarringly out of sync with their inner world.

It's crucial to recognize that family dynamics are not always the sole cause of truancy. Other factors, such as learning disabilities, bullying, or mental health issues, can also contribute. However, the home environment plays a significant role in shaping a teenager's overall well-being and their ability to engage with school. Understanding these complex dynamics is essential for addressing truancy effectively. It's not enough to simply label a student as "truant." We must look beyond the surface, delve deeper into the underlying causes, and offer support that addresses the whole child, not just their attendance record. The whispered halls and empty desks are not merely symptoms of a problem; they are a cry for help, a plea for understanding and connection. By acknowledging the complex interplay of family dynamics and a teenager's struggle with school, we can begin to build bridges of support and create pathways back to belonging.

4.1   Fractured Foundations

Sometimes, the safest place feels like the furthest away. For some teens, that place is home. What happens when the very foundation of your life, your family, is fractured? When the walls that should offer shelter become sources of anxiety, or worse? This isn't about the typical teenage arguments over curfews or phone time. This is about deeper cracks, the kind that run through the core of a family and ripple outwards, impacting every aspect of a young person's life, including their willingness to go to school. School can become a painful reminder of what's missing at home, a stark contrast to the stability and support they crave.

Instability at home takes many forms. It might be parents constantly arguing, the chilling silence of emotional detachment, or the upheaval of divorce and remarriage. Maybe a family member is struggling with addiction, illness, or unemployment, casting a shadow of worry and stress over the household. These situations can create an environment where a teenager feels like they're walking on eggshells, constantly bracing for the next emotional tremor. In these circumstances, school can feel like an unwelcome intrusion, a place where they have to put on a brave face and pretend everything is okay when it's anything but. The energy required to maintain this façade can be draining, leaving little motivation for academics or social interaction.

For some, the instability manifests as a lack of consistent routine and structure. Meals might be unpredictable, bedtimes fluid, and basic needs like clean clothes or a quiet place to study might be unmet. This lack of stability can make it difficult for a teenager to focus on schoolwork, let alone feel motivated to attend. They may be embarrassed to invite friends over, further isolating them from their peer group. The simple act of getting to school on time can become a monumental task when their home life is in disarray. This chaos can spill over into their academic performance, leading to falling grades, missed assignments, and a growing sense of discouragement.

The emotional toll of a fractured family can be immense. Teens might feel responsible for their parents' well-being, taking on adult roles and responsibilities far too early in life. They might feel like they have to mediate conflicts, care for younger siblings, or even contribute financially to the household. This burden of responsibility can be overwhelming, leaving little time or energy for school. The constant worry and stress can lead to anxiety, depression, and difficulty concentrating in class. School, instead of being a place of learning and growth, becomes another source of stress and anxiety.

Sometimes, the fractures are less visible, hidden beneath a veneer of normalcy. A family might appear functional from the outside, but internally, there's a lack of emotional connection and support. Perhaps communication has broken down, replaced by silence and resentment. Maybe a parent is emotionally unavailable due to their own struggles, leaving the teenager feeling unseen and unheard. This emotional neglect can be just as damaging as more overt forms of dysfunction. It can lead to feelings of worthlessness, low self-esteem, and a deep sense of loneliness. School can become a place to escape this emotional void, but also a reminder of the connection they lack at home.

It's important to remember that every family's story is unique and complex. There's no single definition of a "fractured foundation," and the impact on each individual teenager varies greatly. Some teens develop remarkable resilience in the face of adversity, finding ways to cope and even thrive despite their challenging home lives. Others struggle deeply, turning inwards or seeking solace in unhealthy coping mechanisms. Understanding the nuances of these individual experiences is crucial to providing effective support.

The impact of family dynamics on truancy is a complex and multi-faceted issue, often intertwined with other factors such as academic pressure, social isolation, and community challenges. Recognizing the connection between home life and school attendance is the first step towards creating a supportive and understanding environment for teens struggling with these challenges. By acknowledging the invisible burdens they carry and providing resources and support, we can help these students rebuild their foundations and find their way back to a sense of belonging, both at home and at school. This might involve connecting them with school counselors, therapists, or support groups where they can share their experiences and develop coping strategies. It also means fostering a school environment where they feel safe, accepted, and understood, a place where they can find a sense of stability and connection that may be lacking at home.

4.2   The Burden of Responsibility

Sometimes, the weight of the world settles not on broad shoulders, but on young ones, still developing, still learning to navigate the complexities of life. For some teens, the burden of responsibility within their families becomes a significant factor contributing to their absence from school. This isn't about occasional chores or helping with dinner; this is about taking on adult responsibilities - caring for younger siblings, managing household finances, or even holding down a job to contribute to the family income. These responsibilities, while demonstrating in-credible maturity and resilience, often come at a cost. The demands can be overwhelming, leaving little time or energy for schoolwork, ex-tracurricular activities, or simply being a teenager.

Imagine waking up before dawn, not to study for a test, but to get younger siblings ready for school, packing their lunches and ensuring they catch the bus. Picture spending evenings not with friends or on the basketball court, but working a part-time job to help pay the rent or put food on the table. Then, consider the emotional toll - the con-stant worry about family finances, the pressure to be the responsible one, the guilt of potentially letting loved ones down. This is the reality for many teens facing the burden of family responsibilities. It's a reality that often pulls them away from the classroom, not out of apathy or defiance, but out of necessity and a deep sense of obligation.

This heavy load can manifest in various ways. Some teens might miss school entirely to care for a sick family member or to work extended hours. Others might attend school sporadically, their focus divided be-tween classroom lessons and pressing concerns at home. They might struggle to keep up with assignments, participate in class, or even stay awake during lectures, exhausted from the demands outside of school. Their grades may suffer, not because they lack intelligence or motiva-tion, but because they simply lack the time and energy to dedicate to their studies.

The emotional impact of this burden can be profound. These young people are often forced to grow up too fast, shouldering responsibilities far beyond their years. They may experience chronic stress, anxiety, and even depression. They might feel isolated from their peers, unable to relate to typical teenage concerns when their own lives are consumed by adult worries. This isolation can further exacerbate their struggles, creating a cycle of disengagement from school and a growing sense of alienation.

This sense of responsibility can also create a complex internal conflict. These teens understand the importance of education, but they also feel a profound duty to their families. They may feel torn between their desire to succeed in school and their obligation to contribute at home. This internal struggle can be incredibly challenging, leaving them feeling overwhelmed and unsure of where to turn. They might be reluctant to confide in teachers or counselors, fearing judgment or misunderstanding.

For educators and other professionals working with teens, understanding the invisible burdens they carry is crucial. Recognizing the signs of family responsibility - from frequent absences and declining grades to withdrawn behavior and signs of stress - is the first step toward providing effective support. Creating a safe and non-judgmental space where teens feel comfortable sharing their struggles is essential. Offering flexible learning options, connecting families with community resources, and providing emotional support can make a significant difference.

Sometimes, the most powerful intervention is simply acknowledging the weight these young people carry. Letting them know they are seen, heard, and valued, can be a powerful step towards helping them navigate their complex circumstances. Remember, these are not simply truant students; they are young caregivers, providers, and protectors, navigating extraordinary challenges with remarkable resilience. Their stories deserve to be understood, their burdens acknowledged, and their futures supported. By offering compassion, understanding, and practical assistance, we can help them not only stay in school but also thrive, despite the weight they carry. It's about recognizing that for some teens, the greatest challenge isn't inside the classroom, but within the walls of their own homes.

It's important to remember that each situation is unique, and there is no one-size-fits-all solution. Open communication, empathy, and a willingness to collaborate with families are essential for developing effective strategies to support these students. Sometimes, the most significant impact comes from simply offering a listening ear and a reassuring presence, reminding these young people that they are not alone in their struggles. It's about recognizing the strength and resilience they possess and empowering them to navigate their challenging circumstances, one step at a time. Ultimately, the goal is to help them find a balance between their family responsibilities and their educational aspirations, ensuring they have the opportunity to build a brighter future for themselves and their families.

4.3 Seeking Sanctuary

Home isn't always a haven. For some, it's a source of constant stress, a battleground of unspoken tensions, or a place of quiet neglect. When the walls that should offer comfort become suffocating, when the familiar faces bring not solace but anxiety, school can feel like an insurmountable hurdle. The very idea of facing another day within those familiar halls, of navigating the social complexities and academic pressures, can become overwhelming. Truancy, in these cases, isn't about defiance, but about desperately seeking a different kind of sanctuary. It's a search for respite, a desperate attempt to carve out a space of temporary peace amidst the turmoil.

The weight of domestic responsibilities can be crushing for a teenager. Caring for younger siblings, managing household chores, or even contributing financially to the family's survival can leave little time or energy for schoolwork. The constant pressure to meet these demands can overshadow the importance of education, creating a sense of being trapped between competing obligations. The exhaustion, both physical and emotional, can make attending school feel like an impossible task. These young people are often forced to make difficult choices, sacrificing their education to address immediate family needs.

Sometimes, the sanctuary sought isn't a physical place but a mental escape. The pressures at home, whether due to financial instability, parental conflict, or illness, can create an environment of constant anxiety. This anxiety can manifest in various ways, making it difficult to concentrate, sleep, or even leave the house. School, with its demands and social interactions, can become a trigger for this anxiety, leading to avoidance as a coping mechanism. The classroom transforms from a place of learning into a source of overwhelming dread.

The dynamics of a dysfunctional family can be incredibly complex and deeply impactful on a young person's life. Emotional neglect, verbal abuse, or even physical violence can create deep emotional scars. These experiences can erode a teenager's sense of self-worth, making it difficult to believe in their ability to succeed academically or socially. School can become a painful reminder of their perceived inadequacies, a place where they feel exposed and vulnerable. Truancy, in these circumstances, can be a form of self-preservation, a way to avoid further emotional pain.

For some, the sanctuary they seek is simply a space to be unseen, unheard, and undisturbed. Home life can be chaotic and overwhelming, leaving little room for personal space or quiet reflection. The constant noise, activity, and lack of privacy can make it impossible to concentrate on schoolwork or simply decompress after a long day. These teenagers often crave solitude, a place where they can escape the demands and distractions of their home environment. Truancy can provide a temporary reprieve, a chance to reclaim a sense of personal autonomy.

The search for sanctuary can also lead to unexpected places. Some teenagers find solace in the company of others who understand their struggles, forming bonds with peers who share similar experiences. These friendships can provide a sense of validation and belonging, offering a much-needed support system outside of the family. While these connections can be positive, they can also reinforce patterns of truancy if the group dynamic encourages avoiding school. The need for acceptance and connection can sometimes outweigh the importance of education.

It's important to recognize that truancy stemming from challenging home environments is often a cry for help, a silent signal of deeper underlying issues. These young people aren't simply rebellious or lazy; they are struggling to cope with difficult circumstances that are often beyond their control. Understanding the complex interplay of family dynamics and the individual's emotional and psychological needs is crucial in addressing truancy effectively. Offering support, resources, and a non-judgmental ear can make a significant difference in helping these teenagers find the sanctuary they seek and reconnect with their education.

The search for sanctuary is a deeply personal journey. It's a testament to the human spirit's resilience and its innate need for safety, comfort, and connection. Recognizing the complexities of this search is the first step towards offering meaningful support and helping these vulnerable young people find their way back to a place of belonging, both within themselves and within the wider community. It requires empathy, understanding, and a willingness to look beyond the surface behaviors to address the root causes of their struggles. Ultimately, creating a safe and supportive environment, both at home and at school, is essential for these teenagers to thrive and reach their full potential.

5 Beyond the School Walls: Community Factors

The weight of poverty casts a long shadow over a child's education. For many students, the challenges extend far beyond the classroom, into communities grappling with economic hardship. Imagine living in a neighborhood where access to nutritious food is a constant worry. Where stable housing is a privilege, not a right. Where the constant stress of making ends meet permeates every aspect of family life. In these circumstances, school can feel like a distant priority, a world apart from the immediate struggles of survival. The focus shifts from textbooks and tests to more pressing concerns: where the next meal will come from, whether the lights will stay on, how to navigate the complexities of a system that often feels designed to keep them down. This chronic stress can manifest in a variety of ways, affecting a student's physical and mental health, their ability to concentrate, and ultimately, their engagement with school. When basic needs aren't met, the pursuit of education can feel like an insurmountable hurdle.

This struggle is further compounded by a lack of resources within these communities. Imagine schools with outdated textbooks, limited access to technology, and overcrowded classrooms. Visualize after-school programs slashed due to budget cuts, leaving children with fewer opportunities for enrichment and support. Picture libraries closing their doors, limiting access to vital information and educational resources. These resource deserts create a significant disadvantage for students already facing immense challenges. They are denied the tools and opportunities they need to succeed, perpetuating a cycle of inequality that can be difficult to break. This lack of investment in these communities sends a powerful message to the young people living there: that their education is not valued, that their potential is not recognized, and that their futures are not a priority.

The impact of poverty extends beyond material deprivation. It erodes the social fabric of a community, weakening support systems that are crucial for a child's development. Imagine neighborhoods with high crime rates, where fear and mistrust are pervasive. Picture families struggling with unemployment, unable to provide the stability and security that children need to thrive. Envision communities lacking access to quality healthcare, leading to untreated health issues that can impact a student's ability to learn and attend school regularly. These social and environmental factors create a cumulative burden that weighs heavily on children, making it even harder for them to succeed in school.

For many students from low-income communities, the idea of going to college can feel like a distant dream. The financial burden of higher education can seem insurmountable, especially for families struggling to meet their basic needs. The lack of college-going culture in some communities can also create a sense of isolation for students who aspire to higher education. They may lack role models who have successfully navigated the college application process, and they may face pressure from peers or family members who prioritize immediate employment over long-term educational goals. This can create a sense of hopelessness and resignation, leading students to disengage from school and abandon their dreams of a brighter future.

The intersection of poverty and lack of resources creates a complex web of challenges for students. They often face discrimination and stigma based on their socioeconomic background, which can further erode their self-esteem and sense of belonging. They may be labeled as "troubled" or "disengaged" when in reality they are simply struggling to cope with circumstances beyond their control. This mislabeling can lead to disciplinary actions that further alienate them from school, pushing them further down a path of truancy and disengagement. It is crucial to recognize that these students are not inherently problematic; they are simply navigating a system that is often stacked against them. Furthermore, the lack of access to quality healthcare can have a significant impact on student attendance and academic performance. Untreated physical and mental health conditions can lead to chronic absenteeism, making it difficult for students to keep up with their coursework. Students living in poverty may also lack access to mental health services, which can be crucial for coping with the stress and trauma associated with poverty. This lack of access to healthcare exacerbates the challenges these students face, creating additional barriers to their educational success.

The long-term consequences of truancy related to community factors can be devastating. Students who chronically miss school are more likely to drop out, limiting their future opportunities and perpetuating the cycle of poverty. They are also more likely to experience negative health outcomes, encounter the justice system, and struggle with unemployment. It is essential to address the root causes of truancy, not just the symptoms, by investing in communities and providing students with the support they need to succeed. This requires a multi-pronged approach that addresses the social, economic, and environmental factors that contribute to truancy.

Building stronger communities is key to breaking the cycle of poverty and improving educational outcomes for all students. This involves creating safe and supportive environments, investing in affordable housing, expanding access to healthcare and mental health services, and creating economic opportunities for families. It also means providing schools with the resources they need to effectively serve students from low-income backgrounds, including smaller class sizes, qualified teachers, and comprehensive support services. By investing in communities, we can create a more equitable education system that provides all students with the opportunity to reach their full potential.

5.1 Poverty's Grip

The chill wind whipped through the gaps in Maria's worn coat, a constant reminder of the cold that permeated her life, far beyond the physical. Her family's small apartment, with its drafty windows and perpetually rumbling radiator, offered little respite. Heat was a luxury they couldn't consistently afford, just like new clothes, reliable transportation, and sometimes, even food. This constant struggle for basic necessities cast a long shadow over Maria's school life. Concentrating on quadratic equations felt impossible when your stomach growled with hunger. Participating in class discussions felt pointless when you were worried about the overdue rent notice taped to your refrigerator door. School, a place meant for learning and growth, felt increasingly distant, a world apart from her daily realities.

The weight of poverty extended beyond the material. Maria noticed the subtle ways it set her apart from her classmates. Their crisp, new sneakers compared to her scuffed hand-me-downs. Their casual chatter about weekend trips and after-school activities contrasted sharply with her silence. She couldn't join them for pizza after the basketball game or contribute to the class trip fund. These seemingly small things created an invisible barrier, a constant reminder of her family's financial struggles. Shame gnawed at her, a feeling compounded by the fear of being judged, of being seen as "different."

This difference wasn't just perceived; it manifested in tangible ways. Lacking access to a computer and reliable internet at home, Maria struggled to complete assignments that required online research. The library, while a valuable resource, wasn't always accessible due to its limited evening hours and her family's reliance on public transportation. Falling behind in her studies became a vicious cycle. The further she slipped, the more discouraged she felt, and the less motivated she was to attend school. Truancy, once a distant thought, began to feel like a viable option, a temporary escape from the constant pressure.

The school itself, while intended to be a haven, often felt like another source of stress. The free lunch program, though essential, sometimes became a source of embarrassment. Maria felt the sting of curious glances as she stood in the designated line, a stark reminder of her family's circumstances. School supplies, often taken for granted by her peers, were another source of anxiety. A broken pencil, a missing notebook - these small things could derail her entire day, leaving her feeling exposed and inadequate.

The lack of resources extended beyond the classroom. Extracurricular activities, a vital part of the high school experience, were largely inaccessible to Maria. The sports teams required expensive equipment and participation fees. The school clubs often involved off-campus trips and social gatherings that her family couldn't afford. These missed opportunities further isolated her, reinforcing the sense that she didn't quite belong. School, instead of being a place of connection and opportunity, became a constant reminder of what she lacked.

This sense of deprivation seeped into her relationships with teachers and counselors. While some were understanding and supportive, others seemed oblivious to the challenges she faced. Their well-intentioned advice about time management and study habits felt hollow, failing to acknowledge the underlying realities of her life. Explaining the complexities of her situation felt exhausting, a burden she often chose to avoid, leading to misunderstandings and further disconnection.

The constant stress and anxiety took a toll on Maria's mental and emotional well-being. She struggled to sleep, plagued by worries about her family's finances and her own academic struggles. Her appetite fluctuated wildly, swinging between periods of ravenous hunger and a complete lack of interest in food. The joy she once found in learning, in the simple act of discovering new ideas, had been replaced by a pervasive sense of hopelessness.

This hopelessness, in turn, fueled her truancy. Skipping school became a coping mechanism, a way to temporarily escape the pressures she faced. The quiet solitude of her bedroom, though far from ideal, offered a temporary reprieve from the constant reminders of her family's poverty. Each absence, however, further complicated her situation, widening the gap between her and her education, deepening her sense of isolation, and solidifying the grip of poverty on her life. The temporary relief offered by truancy ultimately trapped her in a cycle of disadvantage, making the path back to school, and to a brighter future, increasingly difficult to navigate. The weight of poverty, both tangible and intangible, threatened to crush her spirit and steal her dreams.

5.2 Lack of Resources

Imagine a student arriving at school, stomach churning not from hunger but from anxiety. They're missing essential supplies - pens, paper, maybe even a functioning backpack. Their worn-out shoes pinch, a stark contrast to the pristine sneakers of their peers. This isn't about vanity; it's about the gnawing feeling of being different, of not belonging. This is the reality for many students facing a lack of resources, a reality that can contribute significantly to truancy. When basic needs aren't met, school can feel like an insurmountable obstacle course rather than a place of learning and growth.

The impact of resource scarcity extends far beyond the practical. A student lacking proper clothing might face bullying or social isolation, compounding their feelings of inadequacy. Imagine trying to focus on algebra when you're worried about the holes in your jeans or the whispers in the hallway. The emotional burden becomes a heavy weight, making it harder to engage with studies and fostering a sense of disconnect from the school community. This disconnect can manifest as withdrawal, apathy, or even acting out - all behaviors that can lead to increased absenteeism.

Consider the digital divide, a particularly potent example of resource disparity in the modern age. Access to technology and reliable internet is no longer a luxury but a necessity for academic success. Students without these resources struggle to complete assignments, research projects, and even participate in online learning platforms, putting them at a significant disadvantage. This disparity creates a two-tiered system, further isolating those already struggling and contributing to a sense of hopelessness that fuels truancy. They fall behind, become discouraged, and see little reason to attend a school that feels increasingly irrelevant to their circumstances.

Furthermore, lack of access to nutritious food can have a profound impact on a student's ability to learn and engage in school. Hunger affects concentration, cognitive function, and overall well-being. Students struggling with food insecurity might arrive at school tired, irritable, and unable to focus, making it difficult to keep up with their studies. This constant struggle can erode their motivation and increase their likelihood of missing school altogether. They may feel embarrassed or ashamed of their situation, further contributing to their desire to stay away.

Beyond the individual student, resource scarcity often reflects broader community challenges. Underfunded schools in low-income neighborhoods may lack essential programs, experienced teachers, and adequate support services for struggling students. This creates a cycle of disadvantage, where students from resource-deprived communities face greater obstacles to success and are more likely to become disengaged from school. The school, meant to be a haven, becomes a reflection of the very hardships they are trying to escape.

The lack of affordable transportation presents another significant barrier for students in resource-strained communities. Long distances, unreliable public transit, and the inability to afford even basic transportation options can make attending school a logistical nightmare. Imagine having to walk miles to school, in all weather conditions, just to arrive exhausted and late. This daily struggle can take a toll on a student's motivation and increase their likelihood of missing school entirely. The very act of getting to school becomes a monumental task, overshadowing the potential benefits of education itself.

Moreover, the lack of access to healthcare, including mental health services, can exacerbate the challenges faced by students living in poverty. Untreated physical and mental health issues can lead to increased absenteeism, further marginalizing these students and hindering their educational progress. A student struggling with undiagnosed ADHD, for example, might find it impossible to focus in a traditional classroom setting, leading to frustration, behavioral problems, and ultimately, truancy. Without access to appropriate support, these students are often left to flounder, their potential unrealized.

Addressing the complex issue of truancy requires a multifaceted approach that recognizes and addresses the underlying socioeconomic factors at play. Providing students with access to basic resources – from school supplies and nutritious meals to transportation and healthcare - is not simply an act of charity, but an investment in their future.

It's about creating an environment where all students, regardless of their background, feel valued, supported, and empowered to succeed. By leveling the playing field, we can help break the cycle of disadvantage and ensure that every student has the opportunity to reach their full potential. When students have what they need to thrive, they are more likely to engage with school, build positive relationships, and ultimately, stay in school and graduate, prepared to contribute to their communities and build brighter futures for themselves.

6 Finding a Voice: Student Perspectives

Sixteen-year-old Maya nervously twisted a strand of hair. School had become a battlefield, a constant barrage of anxieties she couldn't navigate. The pressure to achieve academically felt crushing, a weight that made each day heavier than the last. She'd started skipping classes, hiding in the library or wandering the town, anywhere but the classrooms that had become symbols of her perceived inadequacy. She knew it wasn't a solution, but it felt like the only escape.

David, a junior, saw school as a stage for relentless social performance. He felt like an outsider looking in, constantly comparing himself to others. Social media amplified this feeling, presenting a curated reality he could never seem to match. The hallways felt like a minefield of judgment, and the lunchroom, a place of exclusion. His stomach would clench with anxiety each morning, the dread growing until he'd feign illness, choosing the solitude of his room over the perceived rejection of school. He longed for connection, but fear kept him at bay.

Sarah's story was different. She loved learning, thrived on the challenge of new ideas. But her home life was a constant source of stress. Her younger siblings needed care, and her parents struggled to make ends meet. School became a secondary concern, a luxury she couldn't afford. She took on part-time jobs, juggling responsibilities that felt too heavy for her young shoulders. Though her heart ached for the education she was missing, she felt trapped by circumstances beyond her control.

These stories, whispered in quiet corners and shared with trusted confidantes, reveal a common thread: a deep sense of disconnect. Whether stemming from academic pressure, social isolation, or challenging family situations, these students felt like their voices weren't being heard. They were lost in a system that seemed designed for someone else, somewhere else. They yearned for understanding, for a recognition of their unique struggles.

They wished teachers would see beyond the empty desks, beyond the label of "truant." They craved a deeper understanding of the anxieties and pressures they faced, an acknowledgment of the challenges they navigated daily. They dreamed of a school that felt like a sanctuary, a place of support and belonging, rather than a source of stress and alienation. They wanted to be seen, not as problems to be solved, but as individuals with complex needs and untold potential.

Their plea is not for leniency or lowered expectations, but for empathy and understanding. They long for educators to recognize that truancy is often a symptom of a deeper issue, a cry for help masked by silence and absence. They believe that genuine connection can be the catalyst for change, the bridge that leads them back to the classroom and rekindles their passion for learning.

There are glimmers of hope, moments of connection that offer a roadmap forward. A teacher who takes the time to listen, a counselor who offers a safe space to share, a peer who extends a hand of friendship – these small acts of kindness can be transformative. They remind these students that they are not alone, that someone sees their struggle and cares about their well-being.

These students have shown incredible resilience, navigating difficult circumstances with courage and determination. They are not defined by their truancy, but by their strength, their dreams, and their unwavering hope for a brighter future. Their stories are a powerful testament to the human spirit's capacity to overcome adversity. It's time we listen. It's time we learn. It's time we bridge the gap between empty desks and whispered halls, creating spaces where every student feels seen, heard, and valued.

They dream of schools that offer individualized support, recognizing that each student's journey is unique. They envision flexible learning environments that cater to different learning styles and accommodate diverse needs. They yearn for a curriculum that connects to their lives, sparking their curiosity and igniting a passion for learning.

They advocate for mental health resources readily available within schools, providing a safe and accessible space for students to seek support. They believe in the power of peer-to-peer mentorship programs, creating a sense of community and fostering a supportive environment. They emphasize the importance of open communication between students, teachers, and families, building bridges of understanding and fostering collaboration.

Their vision is not utopian, but pragmatic. It is a call for a more compassionate and inclusive educational system, one that recognizes the interconnectedness of academic success, social-emotional well-being, and a sense of belonging. They believe that by addressing the root causes of truancy, we can create schools where every student has the opportunity to thrive.

6.1 Stories of Struggle

Seventeen-year-old Maria traced the chipped Formica tabletop with her finger, the silence of her empty kitchen amplifying the gnawing anxiety in her stomach. School felt like a battlefield. Every day was a new confrontation with the whispers and stares that followed her like a shadow. Her brightly dyed hair, a desperate attempt to carve out some semblance of individuality, had become a target. It was a beacon for the taunts that echoed in the hallways, making her feel exposed and vulnerable. The laughter, meant for others, always seemed to sting her the most. It felt personal, a constant reminder of her perceived otherness. The weight of these daily battles eventually became too much.

The classroom, once a place of potential, transformed into a source of dread. The escape offered by empty desks and whispered halls felt like a fragile sanctuary, a temporary reprieve from the relentless pressure. Fifteen-year-old David sat hunched on his bedroom floor, headphones blasting music to drown out the arguing voices that seeped through the thin walls. Home wasn't a haven. It was a constant source of stress, a battleground of unspoken resentments and simmering tensions. He'd learned to disappear, to become invisible within his own family, slipping out the back door before anyone noticed his absence. School was an extension of that invisibility, a place where he could blend into the background, unnoticed and undisturbed. The anonymity offered a strange comfort, a shield against the turmoil that awaited him at home. He knew he was falling behind, but the thought of facing another day of judgment, both at home and at school, was paralyzing.

Sixteen-year-old Sarah stared at her reflection, barely recognizing the hollow-eyed girl staring back. The responsibility of caring for her younger siblings after school weighed heavily on her. Her mother worked double shifts, and Sarah had become the default caregiver, juggling homework with dinner preparations and bedtime stories. School felt like an impossible luxury, a selfish pursuit that stole precious time from her family obligations. The guilt of prioritizing her own education over her family's immediate needs was a constant battle. The whispered halls became her escape route, a necessary sacrifice she made to keep her family afloat. The empty desks were a symbol of her divided loyalties, a painful reminder of the difficult choices she faced every day. These stories, whispered confessions shared in hushed tones, paint a stark picture of the hidden struggles faced by many teenagers. They are not simply skipping school. They are seeking refuge from overwhelming pressures, navigating complex family dynamics, and grappling with the isolating realities of social ostracization. Maria's story highlights the devastating impact of bullying, how the relentless cruelty of peers can transform a place of learning into a source of fear and anxiety. David's experience reveals the turmoil of a dysfunctional home environment, where school becomes a secondary concern in the face of more immediate survival needs. Sarah's narrative underscores the heavy burden of responsibility shouldered by many young people, forcing them to make agonizing choices between their education and their families.

These are not isolated incidents. They are representative of a larger crisis, a silent epidemic of disengagement that demands our attention. Each empty desk represents a story untold, a silent plea for help lost in the cacophony of the school day. These students are not delinquents. They are not lazy. They are struggling. They are trying to navigate a world that often feels overwhelming, a world that doesn't always see their pain or hear their silent cries for help. The whispered halls are their refuge, a temporary escape from the pressures they face. But these hallways are also a dead end, leading them further away from the opportunities and support they so desperately need.

The stories of Maria, David, and Sarah are a call to action. They are a reminder that truancy is not simply a disciplinary issue. It is a symptom of deeper, more complex problems that require empathy, understanding, and a willingness to address the root causes of student disengagement. We must move beyond simplistic labels and punitive measures. We must create a culture of support, where students feel safe, seen, and heard. We must recognize that the empty desks and whispered halls are not simply spaces of absence. They are spaces of unspoken need, filled with the silent stories of struggling teens waiting to be heard. They are a stark reminder of the human cost of disengagement and a powerful call for a more compassionate and inclusive approach to education. The responsibility lies with us to listen to these stories, to understand the struggles behind the silence, and to create a system that supports all students on their journey to belonging and success.

6.2   A Plea for Change

We've talked about the pressures, the isolation, the struggles at home, and the lack of resources. We've heard stories of students lost in the system, their cries for help often unheard, their potential untapped. Now, we stand at a crossroads. This isn't just a collection of anecdotes; it's a call for action. It's a plea, echoing from the empty desks and whispered halls, for a fundamental shift in how we approach truancy. We must move beyond simply identifying the problem and delve into creating meaningful, sustainable solutions. We must listen, truly listen, to the voices of those who are struggling and allow their experiences to guide us.

This requires a change in perspective. Truancy isn't a disciplinary issue; it's a symptom of deeper, more complex problems. It's a signal flare sent up by a student in distress, a desperate attempt to communicate a need that isn't being met. Punishing the student for this signal only exacerbates the underlying issues, pushing them further into the shadows. Instead, we must ask ourselves: what are these students trying to tell us? What needs are going unmet that are driving them away from the very institution designed to nurture and support them? Are they overwhelmed by academic pressure? Are they struggling with social isolation? Are they facing challenges at home? Are they lacking access to essential resources? These are the questions we must grapple with if we truly want to make a difference.

We must move away from a reactive approach to truancy and embrace a proactive one. This means implementing early intervention programs that identify at-risk students and provide them with the support they need before they disengage from school entirely. These programs should address the root causes of truancy, whether it's academic struggles, social-emotional challenges, or family difficulties. They should offer individualized support tailored to the specific needs of each student, recognizing that there is no one-size-fits-all solution. We need to invest in counselors, social workers, and other support staff who can build relationships with students, provide guidance and mentorship, and help them navigate the challenges they face.

Creating a welcoming and inclusive school environment is paramount. Schools should be safe havens where students feel respected, valued, and supported. This means fostering a culture of kindness and empathy, where bullying and harassment are not tolerated. It means providing opportunities for students to connect with one another and build positive relationships. Extracurricular activities, clubs, and peer support groups can provide a sense of belonging and help students find their niche within the school community. It's about creating a space where every student feels seen, heard, and understood.

Furthermore, we must recognize the crucial role of families in addressing truancy. Schools should work collaboratively with parents and guardians to understand the challenges students are facing at home. This may involve providing resources and support to families struggling with financial hardship, domestic violence, or other difficulties. Open communication between schools and families is essential to ensure that everyone is working together to support the student's well-being. Parent education programs can empower families with the knowledge and skills they need to support their children's academic and social-emotional development.

Addressing truancy requires a collaborative effort. Schools, families, and communities must work together to create a system of support that wraps around struggling students. We need to invest in programs and resources that address the root causes of truancy, rather than simply treating the symptoms. This requires a commitment from policymakers, educators, and community leaders to prioritize the needs of our most vulnerable students. It requires a willingness to listen to their voices, understand their experiences, and act on their behalf.

Finally, we must remember that behind every statistic about truancy is a child with hopes, dreams, and potential. These are not just empty desks; they represent unrealized futures. By addressing the root causes of truancy and creating a system of support that empowers students to succeed, we can help them reclaim their education, unlock their potential, and build brighter futures. This is not just a plea for change; it's an investment in our collective future. It's a recognition that every child deserves the opportunity to thrive, and it's our responsibility to create a world where they can. The whispered halls can become vibrant spaces of learning and connection. The empty desks can be filled with engaged students eager to learn and grow. The change starts with us.

6.3   Hope on the Horizon

It's not about erasing the past. The experiences that led you here, the missed classes, the isolation, the whispered anxieties - they're part of your story. They've shaped you. But they don't define your future. Imagine a horizon. Think of the vastness, the potential stretching out before you. That's where we're focusing now: on the possibilities, on reclaiming your education, on rebuilding connections, and on rediscovering your own strength. This is about finding your path forward.

One of the first steps is often the hardest: acknowledging where you are. Maybe you feel lost, disconnected, or overwhelmed. Maybe you carry a weight of regret or a fear of judgment. It's okay to feel these things. Acknowledging these emotions, giving them space without letting them consume you, is a vital part of moving forward. Think of it like clearing the ground before planting a garden. You need to remove the debris to make room for new growth.

Next, consider what truly matters to you. What are your passions? What kind of future do you envision for yourself? These questions might feel daunting, especially if you've been disconnected from school and your own aspirations for a while. Don't feel pressured to have all the answers right away. Start small. Think about activities you enjoyed as a child, subjects that sparked your curiosity, or careers that seem intriguing. Exploring these interests can rekindle a sense of purpose and direction.

Remember that re-engaging with education doesn't necessarily mean jumping back into a full school schedule overnight. There are alternative paths, flexible options designed to accommodate individual needs and circumstances. Evening classes, online programs, vocational training, and independent study programs can provide a more gradual transition back into learning. Explore these possibilities, talk to counselors, and find a path that aligns with your learning style and goals.

Reconnecting with others can also play a crucial role in finding your way back. Perhaps you've withdrawn from friends and family during your period of truancy. Reaching out can be challenging, but it's often the first step towards rebuilding vital support systems. Start with small gestures - a text message, a phone call, a shared meal. Remember, genuine connections are built on trust and mutual understanding. Be honest about your struggles, but also express your desire to reconnect. Building a support network extends beyond personal relationships. School counselors, mentors, and community organizations can provide invaluable guidance and resources. These individuals are trained to listen without judgment, offer practical advice, and connect you with the support you need. Don't hesitate to reach out. They are there to help you navigate this journey.

Think of your education as a journey, not a race. There will be setbacks, moments of doubt, and times when you feel like giving up. That's normal. The key is to focus on your progress, no matter how small it seems. Celebrate each milestone, acknowledge your resilience, and remember that every step forward is a victory.

Cultivate self-compassion. You've been through a difficult time. Treat yourself with the same kindness and understanding you would offer a friend in a similar situation. Recognize that healing takes time, and be patient with yourself throughout the process.

This journey is about more than just returning to school; it's about reclaiming your future. It's about discovering your strengths, reconnecting with your passions, and building a life filled with purpose and belonging. The path ahead may not always be easy, but with courage, determination, and the right support, you can navigate it successfully. The horizon holds immense promise. Reach for it. Believe in your ability to create a brighter future. This is your time to rise. This is your time to shine.

6.4   Breaking the Silence

Silence isn't always golden. Sometimes, it's a heavy cloak, suffocating the very words we need to speak. For students struggling with truancy, silence can become a default setting, a way to cope with overwhelming feelings of anxiety, isolation, or fear. Breaking that silence, though difficult, is often the first step towards finding a path back to connection and belonging. This chapter is about finding your voice, about understanding the power of your own words, and about recognizing that you don't have to navigate this alone.

Sharing your story can feel incredibly vulnerable. It means exposing the parts of yourself you've worked hard to keep hidden, the parts that feel bruised and tender. You might worry about judgment, about not being believed, or about making things worse. These fears are valid, but they shouldn't hold you captive. Think of it this way: your story is a key. It unlocks understanding, empathy, and ultimately, solutions. When you share your experiences, you're not just helping yourself; you're helping others who feel the same way, letting them know they aren't alone in the darkness.

There are different ways to break the silence. Talking to a trusted adult

- a parent, counselor, teacher, or mentor - can be a powerful first step. Sometimes, just having someone listen without judgment can make a world of difference. If you're not comfortable talking face-to-face, consider writing a letter or journaling. Putting your feelings into words, even if no one else sees them, can help you process what you're going through and gain clarity. Remember, the goal isn't to have all the answers; it's to start the conversation.

For some, connecting with peers who have experienced similar struggles can be incredibly validating. Peer support groups or online forums can provide a safe space to share experiences and offer mutual encouragement. Hearing other students' stories can help you realize that you're not the only one feeling lost or overwhelmed. These shared experiences can foster a sense of community and empower you to advocate for change together. There's strength in numbers, and knowing you're part of a larger group can make the process of seeking help less daunting.

Breaking the silence also means becoming an active participant in your own education. If you're struggling with specific issues at school - bullying, academic pressure, or a lack of support - talk to someone who can help. This could be a school counselor, a teacher, or even a trusted administrator. Don't be afraid to advocate for your needs. You have the right to feel safe and supported in your learning environment. Speaking up about your challenges is a sign of strength, not weakness. Finding your voice doesn't necessarily mean shouting from the rooftops.

It can be a quiet act of self-advocacy, a whisper in the right ear, or a written plea for understanding. The important thing is to find a way to express yourself that feels safe and authentic. It might take time to find the right words and the right person to confide in. Be patient with yourself. The process of breaking the silence is a journey, not a destination.

Your experiences, though painful, hold valuable lessons. By sharing your story, you can contribute to creating a more supportive and understanding school environment for everyone. You can help break down the stigma surrounding truancy and encourage open conversations about the challenges students face. Your voice matters. Your experiences matter. And you deserve to be heard. Don't let fear keep you silent any longer. Breaking the silence, even in a whisper, can be the catalyst for profound change, both within yourself and within your community. Start small, start where you are, and know that there are people ready to listen and support you on your journey. Your voice is a powerful tool. Use it.

The courage it takes to break the silence shouldn't be underestimated. It can feel like standing on a precipice, ready to take a leap into the unknown. But on the other side of that fear lies the possibility of connection, healing, and ultimately, belonging. Remember, you are not defined by your struggles. You are defined by your resilience, your courage, and your willingness to speak your truth. Embrace the power of your voice, and know that you are not alone in this journey. There are people who care, people who want to help, and people who believe in your ability to overcome these challenges. The first step is breaking the silence. The next step is finding your path forward, knowing you have the support and strength to navigate whatever comes next. Trust in yourself, trust in the power of your voice, and trust that brighter days are ahead. You deserve to be heard. Your story matters.

6.5 Paths to Reconnection

Reconnecting with school isn't about snapping back to how things were. It's about forging a new path, one that acknowledges the reasons for disengagement in the first place. This requires a shift in perspective, a willingness to rebuild trust, and a commitment to open communication. Think of it as tending a garden that's been neglected. You can't just expect plants to thrive without addressing the underlying issues - poor soil, lack of sunlight, or insufficient water. Similarly, returning to school requires nurturing the roots of your connection to it. This means understanding your individual needs, identifying the barriers that led to truancy, and actively working to overcome them.

Start by honestly assessing what led to your disconnection. Was it academic pressure, social anxieties, family issues, or something else entirely? Pinpointing the source of your disengagement is crucial. Imagine a tangled ball of yarn. You can't unravel it without finding the loose end. Once you identify the root cause, you can begin to untangle the complexities and find a way forward. Perhaps you felt overwhelmed by the workload. Maybe you felt isolated and unseen. Or perhaps home life made it difficult to focus on school. Whatever the reason, acknowledging it is the first step toward healing and re-engaging.

Reach out to someone you trust - a counselor, teacher, family member, or friend. Sharing your struggles can feel vulnerable, but it's often the catalyst for change. Think of it as letting in fresh air to a stuffy room. Keeping your feelings bottled up only intensifies them. Talking to someone provides perspective, validation, and a sense of shared experience. A trusted adult can offer guidance, support, and practical strategies for navigating the challenges you face. They can also act as advocates, helping you communicate your needs to the school and facilitating your reintegration.

Explore the resources available within your school and community. Many schools offer support services such as tutoring, counseling, and mentoring programs. These resources can provide academic assistance, emotional support, and a sense of belonging. Think of them as tools in a toolbox. You wouldn't try to build a house with just a hammer. Similarly, addressing truancy requires a variety of tools and strategies. Community centers, youth organizations, and online platforms can also offer valuable resources and connections. Don't hesitate to explore these options and find what works best for you.

Consider creating a gradual re-entry plan. Returning to school full-time after an extended absence can feel daunting. A phased approach can ease the transition and build confidence. Perhaps you start with a few classes or attend school for a shorter day. Think of it as dipping your toes into a pool before diving in headfirst. A gradual re-entry allows you to acclimate to the school environment, rebuild relationships, and regain a sense of routine. It also allows you to identify any remaining challenges and adjust your plan accordingly.

Focus on building positive relationships with teachers and classmates. Connecting with others creates a sense of belonging and makes the school environment feel less isolating. Think of it as weaving a tapestry. Each thread represents a connection, and together they create a strong and vibrant whole. Engage in class, participate in extracurricular activities, and reach out to classmates. Even small interactions can make a big difference in building a sense of community.

Remember that reconnection is a journey, not a destination. There will be setbacks and challenges along the way. Be patient with yourself, celebrate small victories, and don't be afraid to ask for help when you need it. Think of it as climbing a mountain. The path may be steep and winding, but the view from the top is worth the effort. Every step forward, no matter how small, is a step in the right direction. By focusing on your strengths, seeking support, and celebrating your progress, you can pave your own unique path to reconnection and rediscover the value of education. This is your journey, and you have the power to shape it.

7 Bridging the Gap: Solutions and Support

Truancy isn't simply about missing school; it's a symptom of deeper disconnections. Addressing these disconnections requires a multifaceted approach, one that acknowledges the interwoven nature of academic pressures, social dynamics, family situations, and community influences. It requires building bridges between students and the support systems designed to help them thrive. One of the most powerful tools in combating truancy is early intervention. Think of it as a preventative measure, like catching a small crack in a bridge before it becomes a major structural issue. Early intervention programs identify warning signs - declining grades, increased absences, changes in behavior - and provide targeted support before a student becomes chronically truant. This might involve individualized tutoring, counseling services, or connecting families with community resources. The key is to address the root causes early, before the problem escalates.

Mentorship programs can play a crucial role in fostering a sense of belonging and connection for students at risk of truancy. A mentor – whether a teacher, community member, or older student – can provide individualized guidance, support, and encouragement. This relationship offers a safe space for students to share their struggles, receive personalized advice, and develop a stronger sense of self-worth. Mentors can help students navigate academic challenges, build social skills, and develop coping mechanisms for stress and anxiety. The consistent presence of a caring adult can make a profound difference in a student's life, offering a lifeline when they feel lost or overwhelmed.

Creating inclusive school environments is paramount to addressing truancy. Schools should be places where every student feels welcomed, respected, and valued. This means fostering a culture of kindness and acceptance, where bullying and discrimination are not tolerated. It means providing diverse extracurricular activities that cater to a wide range of interests, so every student can find their niche and connect with their peers. Inclusive schools prioritize social-emotional learning, equipping students with the skills they need to navigate social situations, manage their emotions, and build healthy relationships. When students feel connected to their school community, they are more likely to engage in their education and less likely to become truant.

Beyond these core strategies, addressing truancy often necessitates collaboration between schools, families, and communities. Open communication channels between teachers and parents are essential for identifying and addressing attendance issues early on. Parent support groups can provide valuable resources and emotional support for families struggling with truancy. Community organizations can offer after-school programs, tutoring services, and mental health support, creating a safety net for students and families in need. This collaborative approach ensures that students receive comprehensive support, both inside and outside of school walls.

Truancy interventions must be tailored to individual student needs. There is no one-size-fits-all solution. Some students may be struggling with academic challenges, while others may be facing social isolation or family difficulties. Effective interventions address the specific underlying causes of truancy, rather than simply treating the symptom of absence. This requires careful assessment of each student's situation, involving teachers, counselors, parents, and the student themselves. Individualized plans may include academic support, counseling, mentoring, or connections to community resources. The goal is to provide targeted support that empowers students to overcome the challenges they face and re-engage with their education.

Building resilience is a crucial aspect of truancy prevention and intervention. Resilience refers to the ability to bounce back from adversity, to navigate challenges and setbacks without becoming discouraged or disengaged. Schools can foster resilience by providing students with coping skills training, mindfulness exercises, and opportunities to develop a growth mindset. This empowers students to view challenges as opportunities for growth, rather than as insurmountable obstacles.

When students develop resilience, they are better equipped to handle the inevitable stresses and pressures of school and life, reducing their risk of truancy.

Creating a sense of belonging is fundamental to addressing truancy. Students who feel connected to their school community are less likely to become disengaged and absent. This sense of belonging can be fostered through a variety of strategies, such as creating welcoming classroom environments, promoting positive peer relationships, and offering diverse extracurricular activities. When students feel seen, heard, and valued, they are more likely to thrive academically and socially. Schools can also create opportunities for students to contribute to their school community, through student government, volunteer programs, or peer mentoring. This empowers students to take ownership of their school environment and fosters a sense of shared responsibility.

Empowering students to take ownership of their education is a powerful tool in combating truancy. When students feel invested in their learning, they are more likely to attend school regularly and engage actively in their studies. This can be achieved by providing students with choices in their learning, offering opportunities for project-based learning, and encouraging student-led initiatives. When students have a voice in their education, they are more likely to feel a sense of purpose and motivation. This sense of ownership can transform the school experience from a passive obligation to an active pursuit of knowledge and personal growth.

Addressing truancy requires a holistic approach that considers the complex interplay of individual, family, school, and community factors. It requires a commitment to early intervention, individualized support, and building a sense of belonging for every student. By working together, educators, parents, community members, and students themselves can create a supportive ecosystem that empowers all young people to thrive. This collaborative effort is essential to ensure that no student falls through the cracks and that every young person has the opportunity to reach their full potential. It's about building bridges, not walls, and creating pathways to success for all students.

7.1 Early Intervention

Truancy rarely erupts overnight. It's a gradual disengagement, a slow fade from the classroom, often preceded by subtle shifts in behavior. Recognizing these early warning signs is crucial for effective intervention. These signals can manifest in academic performance, social interactions, and even physical well-being. A sudden drop in grades, even in a single subject, can be a red flag. Perhaps homework assignments are consistently incomplete, or the student appears disengaged and withdrawn during class. While academic struggles can stem from various sources, a marked shift in performance warrants further investigation. Similarly, changes in social behavior, such as withdrawing from friendships, increased irritability, or expressing feelings of loneliness, can indicate underlying issues contributing to school avoidance.

Physical symptoms like frequent headaches or stomachaches, particularly on school days, can also mask emotional distress. Paying attention to these seemingly small changes can make a profound difference in a student's trajectory.

Early intervention hinges on open communication and collaboration. Teachers, parents, and counselors must work together to create a support network around the student. Regular communication between teachers and parents is essential to identify and address emerging patterns of absenteeism. When a student begins to miss school more frequently, a simple phone call or email from a teacher can express concern and open a dialogue with parents. This early contact can uncover underlying reasons for the absences, whether they are related to academic struggles, social anxieties, family issues, or health concerns. Building a strong home-school connection fosters a sense of shared responsibility for the student's well-being and academic success. Parents can provide valuable insights into the student's behavior and emotional state at home, while teachers can offer observations from the classroom environment. This collaborative approach allows for a more holistic understanding of the student's needs.

Creating a supportive school environment is paramount. Students need to feel safe, respected, and valued within the school community. This sense of belonging can be fostered through inclusive classroom practices, anti-bullying initiatives, and peer support programs. When students feel connected to their peers and teachers, they are more likely to engage in their education and less likely to resort to truancy. A positive school climate promotes a sense of ownership and responsibility, empowering students to actively participate in their learning and contribute to the school community. Creating opportunities for student leadership, extracurricular activities, and community involvement can further enhance this sense of belonging and purpose.

Building strong relationships with students is at the heart of effective intervention. Taking the time to connect with students on a personal level, demonstrating genuine care and interest in their lives, can make a significant difference. This can involve simple gestures like greeting students by name, checking in with them individually, and actively listening to their concerns. Creating a space where students feel comfortable sharing their thoughts and feelings without judgment can foster trust and open communication. When students feel heard and understood, they are more likely to seek help when facing challenges and less likely to disengage from school. This supportive relationship can provide a much-needed anchor during difficult times.

Early intervention also requires addressing the specific needs of each student. A one-size-fits-all approach is rarely effective. Some students may benefit from academic support, such as tutoring or individualized learning plans. Others may require counseling to address underlying emotional or social issues. Still others may need access to community resources, such as healthcare or social services. Identifying and addressing the root causes of truancy is essential for creating sustainable solutions. This may involve connecting students and their families with community organizations that offer specialized support services, such as mental health counseling, substance abuse treatment, or family therapy. Tailoring interventions to meet the unique needs of each student increases the likelihood of success.

Recognizing the interconnectedness of these factors is key. Truancy is often a complex issue with multiple contributing factors. Addressing these interconnected challenges requires a comprehensive approach that considers the student's academic, social, emotional, and familial context. Collaboration between educators, counselors, parents, and community organizations is essential for creating a web of support around the student. This collaborative approach allows for a more holistic understanding of the student's needs and ensures that interventions are coordinated and effective. By working together, these stakeholders can create a safety net that catches students before they fall through the cracks and helps them reconnect with their education. Early intervention is not merely about addressing attendance issues; it is about investing in the well-being and future success of our students.

7.2   Mentorship Programs

Mentorship programs can be a powerful tool in addressing the complex issue of truancy, offering individualized support and guidance to students who are struggling. These programs pair students with mentors who provide a consistent, caring presence in their lives, helping them navigate the challenges that contribute to their disengagement from school. Mentors can be teachers, community members, older students, or other caring adults who are trained to build rapport with young people and understand the multifaceted nature of truancy. A strong mentor relationship can foster a sense of belonging and connection, providing a much-needed anchor for a student who feels adrift. This individualized attention allows mentors to understand the specific reasons behind a student's truancy, whether it's academic struggles, social isolation, family issues, or community-based challenges.

Mentorship goes beyond simply addressing the surface symptoms of truancy. It delves into the root causes, helping students develop coping mechanisms, build resilience, and discover their own strengths. A mentor can be a sounding board, a confidante, and an advocate, providing a safe space for students to express their frustrations and anxieties without judgment. They can help students develop organizational skills, time management strategies, and study habits that can improve their academic performance and reduce the fear of failure. This individualized support can make a significant difference for students who feel lost in the larger school system. Furthermore, mentors can facilitate connections to additional support services within the school and community, acting as a bridge between the student and the resources available.

Effective mentorship programs require careful planning, implementation, and ongoing evaluation. Training for mentors is essential to equip them with the skills and knowledge needed to support students effectively. This training should cover topics such as active listening, building rapport, understanding adolescent development, identifying signs of distress, and working with diverse populations. Mentors also need ongoing support and supervision to ensure they are equipped to handle the challenges they may encounter. Regular meetings, peer support groups, and access to resources can help mentors feel confident and prepared in their roles. The success of a mentorship program relies heavily on the quality of the matches between mentors and mentees. Taking the time to carefully assess the needs and interests of both parties is crucial for building a strong and productive relationship.

In addition to addressing the individual needs of students, mentorship programs can also contribute to a more positive and inclusive school climate. By fostering connections between students and caring adults, these programs can help build a sense of community and belonging. Mentors can model positive behaviors, encourage peer support, and help students develop healthy relationships. They can also provide insights to school staff about the challenges students are facing, informing school-wide strategies to address truancy and improve student engagement. This broader impact can create a ripple effect, benefiting not only the individual mentees but also the school community as a whole.

Evaluation is a critical component of any successful mentorship program. Regularly assessing the program's effectiveness allows for continuous improvement and ensures that it is meeting the needs of both mentors and mentees. Data collection methods can include pre-and post-program surveys, interviews with participants, and tracking of student attendance and academic performance. This data can help identify what aspects of the program are working well and what areas need adjustment. It's also important to gather feedback from mentors and mentees about their experiences, allowing for ongoing refinement and adaptation of the program to best serve the school community. This commitment to evaluation demonstrates a commitment to continuous improvement and maximizes the positive impact of the mentorship program.

The structure and format of mentorship programs can vary depending on the specific needs of the school and the resources available. Some programs may involve weekly one-on-one meetings between mentors and mentees, while others may incorporate group activities or community service projects. The frequency and duration of meetings should be tailored to the individual needs of the student and the availability of the mentor. Flexibility is key to ensuring that the program is accessible and sustainable. Some schools may choose to partner with community organizations to recruit and train mentors, expanding the pool of potential mentors and bringing diverse perspectives to the program. This collaboration can enrich the experience for both students and mentors, fostering stronger connections between the school and the wider community.

The success of mentorship programs lies in their ability to provide personalized support, build strong relationships, and empower students to overcome the barriers to their education. By addressing the root causes of truancy and fostering a sense of belonging, these programs can help create a more supportive and engaging learning environment for all students. They represent an investment not only in individual students but also in the future of the community as a whole. The positive impact of mentorship can extend far beyond the school years, equipping young people with the resilience, skills, and confidence they need to navigate life's challenges and achieve their full potential.

7.3   Creating Inclusive Environments

Schools should be havens, not battlegrounds. Creating a truly inclusive environment requires a shift in perspective, moving beyond simply accommodating differences to fostering a sense of belonging for every student. This means actively dismantling the structures and attitudes that perpetuate exclusion, and building a school culture where every individual feels safe, respected, and valued. It's about moving beyond tolerance to genuine acceptance and celebration of diversity in all its forms. This requires ongoing effort, continuous learning, and a commitment from everyone within the school community.

One crucial aspect of creating an inclusive environment is fostering open communication. Students need to feel comfortable sharing their experiences, thoughts, and concerns without fear of judgment or reprisal. This requires establishing clear communication channels, creating safe spaces for dialogue, and actively listening to student voices. Teachers and staff must be trained to recognize and address microaggressions, bias, and discriminatory behavior. It's about creating a culture of respect where everyone feels empowered to speak up and be heard.

Beyond communication, inclusive environments must prioritize accessibility. This goes far beyond simply providing ramps and elevators. It means ensuring that all students have equal access to learning opportunities, regardless of their physical, cognitive, or emotional needs. This may involve providing individualized support, adapting curriculum and teaching methods, and creating flexible learning environments. It's about recognizing that different students learn in different ways and ensuring that everyone has the tools and support they need to succeed.

Furthermore, creating an inclusive environment necessitates addressing the social dynamics within the school. Cliques, bullying, and social isolation can create significant barriers to belonging. Schools need to actively promote positive social interactions, foster empathy and understanding, and provide opportunities for students to connect with one another. This might involve implementing peer mentoring programs, organizing inclusive social events, and creating spaces where students with shared interests can come together. It's about fostering a sense of community where everyone feels like they belong.

Creating a sense of belonging also involves celebrating diversity. This means recognizing and valuing the unique backgrounds, cultures, and experiences of each student. Schools should incorporate diverse perspectives into the curriculum, create opportunities for students to share their cultural heritage, and celebrate cultural events. It's about creating an environment where every student feels seen, understood, and appreciated for who they are.

Another critical aspect of fostering inclusivity is empowering students to be agents of change. This means providing opportunities for student leadership, involving students in decision-making processes, and creating platforms for student activism. When students feel empowered to shape their school environment, they are more likely to feel a sense of ownership and belonging. This could involve establishing student-led diversity and inclusion committees, providing training on anti-bias and anti-bullying strategies, and supporting student-led initiatives that promote inclusivity. It's about fostering a culture of shared responsibility for creating a positive school climate.

Addressing the root causes of exclusion is essential. This requires examining the systemic inequalities that exist within the school and working to dismantle them. This might involve reviewing school policies and practices, addressing biases in curriculum and assessment, and ensuring equitable access to resources and opportunities. It's about creating a level playing field where all students have the chance to thrive.

Building strong relationships between students, teachers, and staff is paramount. When students feel connected to the adults in their school, they are more likely to feel supported and valued. This involves fostering positive teacher-student relationships, providing opportunities for informal interaction, and creating a sense of community within the classroom and the school as a whole. It's about creating a web of support that helps students navigate the challenges of adolescence.

It's important to remember that creating an inclusive environment is an ongoing process, not a one-time fix. It requires continuous reflection, evaluation, and adaptation. Schools should regularly assess their progress, gather feedback from students and staff, and make adjustments as needed. This can involve conducting school climate surveys, holding focus groups, and creating opportunities for ongoing dialogue. Finally, fostering inclusivity requires a commitment to equity. This means recognizing that different students have different needs and providing the necessary resources and support to ensure that everyone has equal opportunities to succeed. This might involve providing targeted interventions for students who are struggling, creating flexible learning pathways, and ensuring that all students have access to the resources they need to thrive. It's about creating a system where every student has the chance to reach their full potential.

www.ingramcontent.com/pod-product-compliance
Ingram Content Group UK Ltd.
Pitfield, Milton Keynes, MK11 3LW, UK
UKHW021407060225
4478UKWH00036B/750

9 798348 485122